ST. LOUIS
CIVIL WAR SITES

and the

FIGHT FOR FREEDOM

T0274697

St. Louis Civil War Sites

and the

FIGHT FOR FREEDOM

PETER DOWNS

THE
History
PRESS

Published by The History Press
Charleston, SC
www.historypress.com

Cover photos by Peter Downs.

First published 2022

Manufactured in the United States

ISBN 9781467152723

Library of Congress Control Number: 2022937943

CONTENTS

Contents

ACKNOWLEDGEMENTS

This book would not have been possible without the enormous work of countless historians who researched and wrote about the Civil War and the people and places in it. I admire their work and am grateful for it.

I am indebted to all the librarians who helped me find materials and information, especially at the St. Louis Public Library Central Library and the Missouri Historical Society Library and Research Center. Both institutions are amazing public resources.

I owe thanks to Chad Rhoad and the staff at The History Press for their advice and assistance on producing this book.

Last but not least, I am thankful for the support and suggestions from my wife and daughters, Maureen, Ashley, Devlin and Bergin.

PART I

PRELUDE TO WAR

Mary Meachum and
Resistance to Slavery

1

FREEDOM CROSSING

On Sunday night, May 20, 1855, an enslaved woman named Esther, along with her two young sons and an enslaved man named Jim Kennerly, made her way to a spot about three and a half miles north of downtown St. Louis, just upriver of Bissell's ferry. She joined other enslaved people[1] waiting for some men with a skiff to take them across the Mississippi River to Illinois and the next stage in their journey to freedom. That site, adjacent to the north riverfront hiking and biking trail, is part of the National Park Service's National Underground Railroad Network to Freedom. It is known as the Mary Meachum Freedom Crossing.

Jim, Esther and her sons, ages six and eight, had escaped from Henry Shaw, a prominent local businessman better known today for creating the Missouri Botanical Garden and Tower Grove Park. Shaw had a townhome at the southwest corner of Seventh and Locust Streets. The site is now a parking lot.

Esther didn't make it very far. Someone had tipped off the St. Louis sheriff to the escape plan. A deputy's posse waited in hiding for the boat at the Illinois landing site. Among them was a bounty hunter hired by Henry Shaw. They may have been motivated by the reward money to spring their trap in Illinois instead of at the meeting place in Missouri. Missouri law authorized payment of $100 to anyone who captured a runaway enslaved person older than twenty outside the borders of the state. If the capture happened within the state, however, the reward was only $25.[2]

This mural by St. Louis Artworks celebrates the location of the Mary Meachum Freedom Crossing, part of the National Park Service's National Underground Railroad Network to Freedom. *Peter Downs*.

The sheriff's party waited until everyone was on the shore and then opened fire. They wounded an African American man from Alton who was helping the enslaved people escape. He died three days later.[3]

Jim Kennerly and some of the others got away, as did the men operating the skiff, whom the *Missouri Republican* called "cowardly abolitionists."[4] Esther, her two boys and two other people seeking freedom were captured, chained and brought back to St. Louis.

Two days later, the St. Louis sheriff arrested Mary Meachum and two other free African Americans, Judah Burrows and Isaac Breckenridge,[5] and charged them with enticing the enslaved people to escape. The penalty for enticing an enslaved person to escape was five to ten years in the state prison.[6] Nine St. Louisans in the 1840s and 1850s were imprisoned in the Missouri State Penitentiary for such "slave stealing," including two African American men and an African American woman.[7]

The *Missouri Republican* reported that one of the men captured on Sunday night fingered Mary as a key organizer of the escape plan.[8] It is impossible to know whether that actually happened, or if the sheriff gave out that story to cover for the informant who had alerted them to the escape plan. Or perhaps the sheriff had other reasons to target Mary. In the event, the prosecutor did not present such a witness at Mary's trial. She was tried before a jury and acquitted on July 19.[9] Prosecutors dropped all charges against Isaac the next day.

The escape attempt was so unusual for its size that the *Missouri Democrat* sensationalized it as a "stampede."[10] Very few enslaved people escaped from Missouri—no more than six to ten a year, according to one study[11]—and most who did so managed it in ones or twos.

Prosecutors may have targeted Mary because she long had been a thorn in the side of slaveholders and white supremacists but always seemed to stay just out of the reach of the law. She and her husband, John Berry Meachum, had established the first church for Black people in St. Louis, an African Baptist church, in 1826. They erected their own church building on Almond Street between Fourth and Fifth Streets in 1842.[12] The site is now underneath a Tums factory.

Many whites viewed African American churches with suspicion, claiming they instilled "fanatical principles" into the minds of slaves.[13] A law enacted in 1847 required the presence of a county official at every religious service in an African American church.[14] Like any other boring duty, however, enforcement probably varied tremendously. Advertisements for the return

The Mississippi River is narrow at the Mary Meachum Freedom Crossing during drier seasons. *Peter Downs.*

The Meachum house and business were on Second Street between St. Charles and Washington in what now is the northwest corner of the Gateway Arch National Park. *Peter Downs.*

of runaway enslaved people in the 1850s often mentioned that the enslaved person had disappeared on a Sunday evening after church service.[15]

Mary and John Berry Meachum were both formerly enslaved people. John Berry, a skilled carpenter, had earned the money to buy his own freedom and then bought Mary. He ran a successful barrel-making business on Second Street between Vine Street and Washington Avenue in addition to the church. He may have done business with the Chouteaus, who dominated trade with Native Americans and outfitted riverboat expeditions going west from an office around the corner from John Berry's shop. River expeditions needed barrels for storing supplies and trade goods.

The Meachums' neighbors in the 1830s included the town's leading citizens: Chouteau clan leader Pierre Chouteau Jr., his sister-in-law Madam August P. Chouteau, General William Clark[16] and, two blocks to the west, the Brants, who put up Senator Thomas Hart Benton whenever he came to town.[17] Besides the house and business in St. Louis, the Meachums also owned a brick house and farm in Illinois.[18] A visitor in 1841 reported that they were said to be worth $55,000 (equivalent to more than $1.6 million in 2020).[19]

Their wealth made the Meachums a target of envy, but it was what they did with it that some whites found objectionable. They bought enslaved people and converted them to indentured servants who gained their freedom when they paid back their purchase price. They had freed twenty enslaved people in that way by 1846.[20] Some of those formerly enslaved people then bought and freed more enslaved people. Since an average of only five to nine enslaved people a year were manumitted in Missouri in the 1840s and 1850s,[21] a significant percentage must have been freed by African American purchasers. John Berry preached that it was the duty of every able-bodied slave to save up to buy his freedom and then save more to buy the freedom of others.[22]

Whites in Missouri were wildly afraid of free African Americans. The state constitution of 1820 even instructed the future legislature to enact laws "to prevent free negroes and mulattoes from coming to, and settling in this state."[23] A law enacted in 1843 required them to post a bond of up to $1,000 (equivalent to over $36,000 in 2020)[24] for a residency license.[25] Other laws restricted the right to meet with or assemble with other African Americans; set curfews; required that children be indentured as servants or apprentices at age seven; and defined occasions for treating free African Americans as runaway slaves and for expelling them from the state.[26] Nevertheless, newspapers and popular meetings often complained that authorities weren't doing enough and demanded action to rid the state of free African Americans.[27]

John Berry sought to navigate through the hysteria by, in part, advocating colonization,[28] which was the idea that former slaves should be transported to some other land to colonize it. Some proponents of colonization advocated a return to Africa and backed the American-supported colony in Liberia.[29] Others advocated for the creation of a U.S.-affiliated colony in Central America. John Berry became an agent of the Missouri Colonization Society, which included some of the most important men in Missouri politics.

John Berry did not publicly support abolition, insurrection or even legal reform of slavery.[30] He endorsed hard work and sober living instead. We do not know if his conservative public statements reflected his beliefs or were meant to reassure whites that he and his actions were not a threat or a kind of protective coloration to hide his real beliefs and any covert activities he might be part of. Many whites, however, were not reassured, and the movement to rid Missouri of free African Americans gained steam during his lifetime.

Mary and John Berry had run afoul of the law at least once before her arrest in 1855. They ran a school for African Americans. John Berry had started it in the early 1820s, when he was a protégé of a white Baptist preacher named John Mason Peck. He continued the practice after Peck ordained

Mary Meachum's Tenth Street homesite is now part of the Eagleton Federal Courthouse. *Peter Downs.*

him, and his wife joined him when they organized their own church, despite a city ordinance that prohibited the education of African Americans.[31] The sheriff shut down their school in 1847 after the state banned any instruction of Blacks or "mulattoes" in reading or writing[32] and jailed the teacher. The Meachums hired lawyers, who were able to free the teacher, and are said to have continued educating Black children, but covertly.[33]

Some historians say John Berry then built a steamboat and moored it in the middle of the Mississippi River outside the jurisdiction of Missouri to house a school, shuttling children by boat out to the steamboat and back.[34] Others disagree, saying that that story mixes up two separate elements in John's life: his ownership of a steamboat and his operation of a school.[35]

John Berry did own a steamboat. According to Gershom Perdue, a Quaker minister who stopped in St. Louis and visited the Meachums in January 1841, John Berry built a steamboat in 1835 and "provided it with a good library."[36] That was a decade before the sheriff shut down the school in St. Louis.

The willingness of the sheriff to operate across state lines, and the willingness of proslavery vigilantes to ignore state boundaries, casts doubt on whether simply mooring the boat in the river would have enabled John Berry to escape the reach of a sheriff or the ire of vigilantes.

John Berry died in 1854 while preaching from his pulpit. He left Mary wealthy and potentially more vulnerable. Following John Berry's death, Mary had trouble with the contractors building her a new home at 67 South Tenth Street between what is now Clark Street and Walnut. The site is now part of the Thomas F. Eagleton U.S. Courthouse. Between January 9 and her arrest on May 22, 1855, the plasterer, painter, carpenter and laborer all filed liens against her new house for nonpayment of debt.[37]

Whether the St. Louis sheriff really had evidence against her in 1855 or just thought it was time to bring her down is not known. Regardless, the confluence of the escape attempt on May 20 and her apparent financial troubles gave him an opportunity to act. Mary stayed strong, however. She beat the charges, settled the debts tied to the mechanics' liens and, a year later, guaranteed residency bonds for three new free African Americans in St. Louis—guarantees that totaled $3,000, equivalent to almost $100,000 in 2020.[38]

2

SIXTH STREET JAIL

Mary Meachum would have been taken to the notorious city jail at Sixth and Chestnut Streets, next to what is now Kiener Plaza, after her arrest. That was the same jail from which a mob of white men nineteen years earlier had dragged Francis McIntosh before tying him to a tree and burning him alive. Contemporary sources placed the tree on Chestnut Street between Seventh and Eighth,[39] currently the site of Peabody Plaza.

Francis McIntosh was a mixed-race man from Pittsburgh who worked as a steward on the steamboat *Flora*. He was arrested on the St. Louis riverfront on April 28, 1836, by Deputy Sheriff George Hammond and Deputy Constable William Mull, ostensibly for obstructing their efforts to arrest another sailor, whether he actively interfered with their efforts or simply ignored a request to help them is unknown. Accounts differ.[40]

The prospects for a Black man arrested in a slave state were not good, but McIntosh cooperated at first. It was after he asked the deputies his likely punishment that he got agitated. Hammond said he'd probably hang. That's when McIntosh tried to break free.[41] He pulled a knife, sliced Hammond across the neck, opening the carotid artery, and stabbed Mull in the abdomen. Mull shouted an alarm, and nearby men gave chase. They cornered McIntosh in a private lot near Fourth and Walnut Streets, where he was arrested and then taken to jail.

A crowd, by some accounts led by some of the town's business and civic leaders,[42] gathered at the jail that evening and demanded McIntosh be put

The Sixth Street Jail as it appeared in an 1870 photo by Emil Boehl. Today, the site is a parking garage with first-floor retail space. *Missouri Historical Society*.

to death. The sheriff ran away, leaving the jail unguarded. The mob broke into the jail and dragged McIntosh out to a nearby locust tree. They chained him to the south side of the tree. They then stacked wood around him and set it on fire.

Accounts of how long McIntosh suffered before he died and the number of people involved in the atrocity differ, but many were written years after the event and years after it had become a stand-in for views on slavery. Elijah Lovejoy, editor of the *St. Louis Observer*, wrote at the time that McIntosh suffered for twenty minutes before dying, during which time he begged someone to shoot him and tried to pray.

The lynching spread fear through the local African American community. One local newspaper, the *Missouri Argus*, editorialized that free African Americans in the city should take the mob action as a "reminder…to be cautious."[43] There was an immediate and dramatic drop in the number of enslaved people filing lawsuits challenging their enslavement. It would take six years before the number of such suits in the circuit court returned to pre-McIntosh levels.[44]

Burning of McIntosh at St. Louis, in April, 1836.

An illustration of Francis McIntosh's lynching from 1840. *Library of Congress.*

That lynching became one of the defining moments of the movement to abolish slavery and sharply split the country. Abolitionists like Theodore Weld and Elizur Wright said the city's acceptance of the gruesome killing illustrated the moral bankruptcy of slavery.[45] The willingness of the mob to break the law to impose its own punishment, and the acquiescence of civil authorities, exposed the threat of slavery to civilized society and the rule of law. However, people sympathetic to slavery described McIntosh as a defiant criminal who deserved what he got. They labeled the men who apprehended him and killed him as heroes and protectors of law and order.

Abraham Lincoln, then a state legislator in Illinois, described the lynching of McIntosh as "revolting to humanity" and "horror-striking." McIntosh "had forfeited his life" by killing the deputies, but it must be taken by the process of law, he said. For, "whenever the vicious portion of population shall be permitted to gather in bands of hundreds and thousands, and burn churches, ravage and rob provision stores, throw printing presses into rivers, shoot editors, and hang and burn obnoxious persons at pleasure, and with impunity; depend on it, this Government cannot last."[46]

His message was that slavery created the environment that permitted and even encouraged such outrages.

The *Missouri Republican*, the leading newspaper in the city, had editorialized the hope that the McIntosh affair would soon be forgotten. It was not to be. The story of the atrocity was told in the city for decades, and the tree where

McIntosh was burned became a pilgrimage site for abolitionists until city leaders had it cut down to discourage such visits.

The lynching of McIntosh remained in St. Louisans' memories for life—a haunting memory for some, a proud one for others. Mayor John Darby would write about it forty-four years later without remorse or apology.[47] Westward-bound travelers would stop at the site for many years afterward and tie a yellow ribbon around the tree in memory of McIntosh.[48] British author Charles Dickens wrote about it to a friend after visiting St. Louis in 1842.[49]

Mary Meachum, who lived through it, certainly would have remembered it.

The sheriff or his deputies also may have taunted her with references to previous "abolitionists" kept in the jail in 1841 and hanged for murder and arson. Four African American men were arrested in April 1841 for murdering two bank employees and torching the bank in an unsuccessful robbery attempt.

City leaders, still smarting at the time from criticism the city received for the McIntosh lynching, wanted to showcase their ability to manage an orderly legal process.[50] They got one of the men, Charles Brown, to confess to being a paid agent of the Ohio Anti-Slavery Society and another, Madison Henderson, to confess to luring enslaved people to run away "to freedom" so that his boss could kidnap them and sell them in the Deep South.[51]

The trial judge arranged for the confessions to be printed in the *Missouri Republican* during the trial. Hamilton Gamble, one of the court-appointed defense attorneys, objected that the confessions were coerced, but the publisher of the *Missouri Republican* claimed that the men reviewed and approved them before publication.[52]

More than twenty thousand people, equal to about three-quarters of the city's population, were said to have turned out for the hanging on July 9, 1841. Steamboat companies scheduled excursions for people from cities up and down the river to attend, and the *Missouri Republican* sold a souvenir confessions booklet.[53]

Whatever truth may have been in the confessions, they were perfectly suited to fit the propaganda aims of proslavery leaders. The confessions showed abolitionists as criminals and enemies of law and government and warned enslaved people not to trust anyone offering to help them escape, because the offer could be a ruse that would place them in a worse situation down South.

Abolitionists tended to dismiss the confessions, but they played well with the proslavery base. The Brown and Henderson confessions gave new energy to a movement against free African Americans in Missouri. In the wake

Peabody Plaza occupies the site where a crowd lynched Francis McIntosh in 1836. *Peter Downs.*

of the trial, the city enacted more stringent regulations on the movement and activities of free African Americans and stepped-up enforcement of existing regulations.[54] The state legislature approved the first new restriction in twenty years on free Blacks entering the state.[55]

Mary's spirits while she was in jail may have been buoyed by visits from African American Baptist minister John Richard Anderson, a former student of the Meachums and a former junior minister in their church. Anderson had the job of cleaning the jail and feeding the prisoners,[56] which put him in a position to minister to enslaved people locked up for suing for freedom, and also to African American prisoners like Mary Meachum. Anderson may have relayed messages between Mary, her codefendants and people outside jail.

MOSES DICKSON AND THE KNIGHTS OF LIBERTY

T he Brown and Henderson Gang confessions cast riverboat routes as a criminal network, an underworld of slaves and African Americans up to no good. Freedom workers like Mary Meachum must have had another view of it.

Decades after the Civil War, Moses Dickson described how he and other riverboat workers used their positions to secretly organize enslaved people to resist the enslavers and sometimes help people escape to freedom.[57]

Dickson said he and eleven other African Americans met in a two-story brick house on the southeast corner of Seventh Street and Green Street (now called Lucas Avenue) on August 12, 1846,[58] to lay the foundation for the Knights of Liberty, a secret society of free and enslaved Blacks aiming to organize an armed insurrection across the South to end slavery. The site is now part of a large building that houses apartments, a hotel and the National Blues Museum.

The founders of the Knights of Liberty hailed from Missouri and eight southern states: Virginia, North Carolina, South Carolina, Tennessee, Georgia, Alabama, Mississippi and Louisiana.[59] They all were steamboat workers. Interstate travel and commerce depended on African American labor to keep the boats moving and livable. Free and enslaved African Americans alike served as deckhands, cabin boys, stevedores and barbers for travelers. Dickson was a barber.[60]

The Knights of Liberty aimed to organize African American communities along their routes of travel, but they also helped enslaved people escape from their enslavers. Dickson told one story of how he helped a mother and

Moses Dickson is memorialized at the African American cemetery he initiated. The cemetery also has an interpretive plaque about African American soldiers in the Civil War. *Peter Downs.*

daughter escape New Orleans by disguising them as a young man and a boy and placing them as crew on a riverboat under a mate who was a member of the Knights. Another time, he and fellow Knights helped a young man escape from Charleston in a box they built with hidden air holes and stocked with food and water. They shipped him to Boston under the watchful eye of crew members who were part of the Knights network.[61]

Mary and John Meachum, as steamboat owners and opponents of slavery, would have been well aware of the opportunities for helping individuals escape slavery provided by a working steamboat, particularly if they could carefully select the crew.

Many African American steamboat workers and levee workers joined the Second African Baptist Church that branched off from the Meachums' church. The Second African Baptist Church began holding services in 1846 near the levee in Liberty Hall at Third Street and Franklin Avenue (then called Cherry Street). The congregation acquired its own building in 1851 at Eighth and Green, one block from the founding place of the Knights of Liberty, largely on the strength of donations from riverboat and levee workers.[62] Dred Scott's wife, Harriet, was a member of the congregation. Members of the church surely paid close attention to her freedom lawsuit.

The St. Louis levee in 1853. River commerce depended on the labor of African Americans. *Missouri Historical Society.*

Dickson said the Scott case was one reason the Knights canceled their rebellion. He claimed they had thousands of men drilling secretly at night in every southern state except Texas and Missouri by 1856.[63] They had planned to issue a call for an uprising sometime between December 1856 and July 1857 and march on Atlanta, Georgia.

Dickson was supposed to issue the call to rise up, but he never did. He said the Dred Scott case and the election of 1856 pointed to a sharpening conflict over slavery among whites. John Frémont, the antislavery candidate of the new Republican Party, came in second in the three-way race for president, garnering one-third of the vote. Even in Missouri, Frank Blair and B. Gratz Brown, two longtime allies and lieutenants of Senator Thomas Hart Benton, abandoned Benton's "don't speak of slavery" policy to come out against slavery. Dickson said he decided to wait and watch the conflict sharpen.[64]

Slave revolts rolled across the South in late 1856 and early 1857 anyway, springing up in Virginia, South Carolina and Florida, spreading across Kentucky and Tennessee to Mississippi, Louisiana, Arkansas and Missouri.

Dickson said the Knights disbanded during the Civil War, but he and the other leaders quickly enlisted on the Union side when given the opportunity to do so.[65] Due to the prominence of African American labor in the riverboat industry, the navy admitted African Americans to its ranks much earlier than did the army and paid African American sailors the same as whites.

Dickson is buried at Father Dickson Cemetery, an African American cemetery he founded at 845 Sappington Road.

LYNCH'S SLAVE PEN SITE

Esther was not taken to the city jail like Mary Meachum after her arrest. She was instead taken to Bernard Lynch's slave pen at 104 Locust Street. She later was sold from there to a slave owner in Vicksburg, Mississippi.[66] The Federal Reserve Bank of St. Louis occupies the former site of the slave pen.

Lynch's slave pen was a two-and-a-half-story structure that included quarters for an overseer as well as cells for enslaved people.[67] Shaw paid Lynch to keep Esther locked in the pen until he sold her. It took Lynch seventy days to arrange the sale. Other slaves, male and female, were locked in the same room with Esther. Each one was shackled. There were bars on the window, and the door was secured with bolts and locks.

Galusha Anderson, then pastor of the local Second Baptist Church, described Lynch's slave pen as it was during a visit by preachers in 1859 in his book *The Story of a Border City during the Civil War*.[68] "The room was in the shape of a parallelogram. It was plastered and had one small window high up near the ceiling. There was no floor but the bare earth. Three backless wooden benches stood next to the walls. There were seven slaves there, both men and women, herded together, without any arrangement for privacy."

Anderson wrote that he was used to seeing men and women handcuffed and chained together in St. Louis and forced to go to the slave pen "under the crack of a driver's whip as though they were colts or calves."[69] Samuel Clemens, better known as Mark Twain, would have been familiar with the sight, too. For a short time, he lived across the street from Lynch's slave

Henry Shaw employed Bernard Lynch, whose office is depicted in this photo, to recapture Hannah after she escaped. *Missouri Historical Society*.

The Federal Reserve Bank Plaza occupies the site of the slave pen where Bernard Lynch held Hannah after recapturing her. *Missouri Historical Society*.

pen. Lynch's pen was near the center of commercial and cultural life in St. Louis, one block east of the celebrated Mercantile Library and two blocks northwest of the famous Planter's House Hotel.

The decade of the 1850s was a time when slavery was strengthening its grip on Missouri and slave laws were getting harsher. Lynch's slave trade grew so much during the decade that he bought another location at Fifth and Myrtle, present-day Broadway and Clark and the site of Ballpark Village. Lynch set this facility aside specifically for children. It was only three blocks from the Meachums' African Baptist Church. Anderson described the trafficking in children as "specially brisk and profitable."[70]

Children sold at the slave pen ranged in age from five to sixteen. Auctions took place every few weeks. The normal regularity of such events contributed to the casual dehumanization of African American people. Anderson recalled witnessing the extreme grief of mothers when they were separated from their children. One of the auction managers assured Anderson there was nothing to worry about, saying it was like a cow getting separated from her calf.[71]

Esther ran away from Henry Shaw, whose townhouse was on the southwest corner of Seventh and Locust. *Missouri Historical Society*.

Shaw specified in his will that his townhouse be moved to the botanical garden he created, where today it is used for administrative offices. *Peter Downs.*

The growing importance of St. Louis in the slave trade in the 1850s was such that a national competitor to Lynch, Lexington, Kentucky–based Bolton, Dickens and Company, expanded to St. Louis in 1855, the same year Mary Meachum was charged with helping people escape enslavement. They had their main office on Chestnut Street between Sixth and Seventh Streets, now part of Kiener Plaza, and a trade office at 52 Second Street, now underneath the Gateway Arch grounds.

Bolton, Dickens and Company was one of the largest slave-trading companies in the nation, with gross sales totaling several million dollars a year (equivalent in 2020 terms to more than $100 million). They specialized in buying enslaved people in states of the Upper South in places like St. Louis and shipping them to the Deep South by way of Memphis.[72]

5

THE GATEWAY ARCH NATIONAL PARK GROUNDS ELIJAH LOVEJOY SITE

Many of St. Louis's leading citizens in 1836 probably agreed with the *Missouri Republican* in wanting to bury and forget the cruel lynching of Francis McIntosh, but Elijah Lovejoy was not one of them. Lovejoy denounced the "mobism" of the McIntosh murder and described the scene in detail in the *St. Louis Observer*,[73] a Presbyterian newspaper largely devoted to religious topics.

Like many moderate opponents of slavery after him, Lovejoy described McIntosh as a "hardened wretch" who "deserved to die—but not thus to die." Nowhere in the article did Lovejoy mention slavery. Rather, he condemned mob justice and called for the city to return to living under law and the U.S. Constitution. In sermons that accompanied the description of the murder, however, Lovejoy described slavery as "a sin" and lamented "the abandonment of virtue…[by] Pro-slavery men."

A grand jury convened at 121 South Fourth Street to investigate the lynching. Judge Luke Lawless seemed less concerned with the crime than he was with Lovejoy. He turned the hearing into an indictment of Lovejoy and anyone who opposed slavery. He told jurors it was up to them to determine if the horrific lynching was the work of a few people—in which case they all ought to be indicted—or the work of many, seized by a "mysterious, metaphysical, and almost electric phrenzy."[74] If the latter, he said, then the case "is beyond the reach of human law."[75]

Lawless said those involved in McIntosh's murder "must already regret what they have done,"[76] and the important question was why they did it. He

Abolitionist Elijah Lovejoy's former home and offices are among the sites occupied by the northern half of the Gateway Arch National Park. *Peter Downs.*

then gave the jury his answer: the mob was aroused not just by McIntosh's killing of Deputy Hammond but also by what he claimed were "similar atrocities…by individuals of Negro blood against their white brethren."[77]

He said that McIntosh's demeanor while being burned to death, his lack of penitence and the curses he hurled at his killers (which suggests that Lawless was part of the mob) showed that McIntosh was influenced by the "incendiary" teachings of abolitionists.[78] He distributed copies of the *Observer* and said that when a Black man hears views like those of the *Observer*, he "then kills and burns for the love of God and in the name of the Divine Redeemer, and rushes on to crime and carnage under the influence of what appears to him a holy impulse and aspiration."[79]

Lawless urged the jury to ignore the lynching of McIntosh and instead look for methods to silence the voices of abolitionism and suppress the press that causes such mischief.[80] This was consistent with his antipathy to the press. He had ruled in a previous case that truth could not be used as a defense against a charge of libel.[81]

The jury, led by John O'Fallon, a slave owner, Missouri's first representative in Congress and one of the wealthiest men in the city, followed Lawless's lead and declined to indict anyone for McIntosh's murder. O'Fallon was the nephew and protégé of another prominent slaveholder, William Clark, the coleader of the Lewis and Clark Expedition and former territorial governor of Missouri.

Afterward, a mob of over two hundred men broke into the office of the *Observer*, just a couple of blocks south of where the Meachums lived. They smashed the press and threw the pieces into the Mississippi River. The Missouri legislature followed the riot by banning "the publication, circulation, and promulgation of the abolition doctrines," with penalties for violating the ban of up to two years in prison and a maximum fine of $1,000. The penalty increased to twenty years in prison after a second offense and life in prison after a third.[82]

Lovejoy moved to Alton, Illinois, after the Lawless riot, but southern Illinois was not much different from St. Louis. Three times, mobs broke into his Alton office and destroyed his printing press.[83] He asked the city council for protection and organized his own security detail when they failed to act. A mob led by prominent citizens then set fire to the building housing Lovejoy's new printing press and shot and killed him when he tried to stop the fire.[84] One of the witnesses to the murder was John Richard Anderson, an African American who set type for Elijah Lovejoy. Anderson had been educated by the Meachums at their Sunday school and later became a minister in their church.[85]

City Attorney Francis Murdoch followed Lovejoy's death by charging Lovejoy's associates with violently and unlawfully resisting an attempt to break up the press, claiming it was their actions with Lovejoy that led to "a breach of the peace."[86] He was assisted in his prosecution of the case by Illinois attorney general U.F. Linder, who told the jury Lovejoy's purpose was "to teach rebellion and insurrection to the slave; to excite servile war; to preach murder in the name of religion…and spread desolation over the face of this land."[87] Lovejoy's associates all were acquitted.

Murdoch then charged eleven men for Lovejoy's murder. It came out at the trial that Mayor John Krum, lawyers, doctors and even the judge presiding over the trial were members of the mob that attacked the warehouse and killed Lovejoy. Krum said he was there to mediate between Lovejoy and slavery supporters. He delivered the mob's final ultimatum to Lovejoy but said he did it as a way to stall for time so that tempers could cool.[88] Linder this time represented the defense, which justified the mob's actions as a legitimate defense against the dangers of an abolitionist press.[89]

Everyone was acquitted.

The killing of a white man shocked parts of the nation in the way that no killing of a Black man had done. John Quincy Adams, former president and

A monument to Elijah P. Lovejoy rises from a hilltop cemetery at 1299 East Fifth Street in Alton, Illinois. *Peter Downs*.

then member of the U.S. House of Representatives, said the news struck like an earthquake.[90] Newspapers across the North condemned Alton, ministers delivered sermons honoring Lovejoy and Northern public opinion shifted against slavery.[91]

New recruits flocked to the antislavery cause as abolitionist speakers pointed to the Lovejoy killing as proof that slavery threatened the rights of white Americans as well as the liberties of Blacks. One, a young man named John Brown, stood at a memorial for Elijah Lovejoy in Hudson, Ohio, and swore that he would devote his life to the destruction of slavery. He later fought slavery in Kansas and led a small uprising in Harpers Ferry, Virginia.[92]

The Lovejoy killing also turned a young lawyer in Vermont named Roswell Field against slavery.[93] Field later moved to St. Louis and became one of the lawyers representing Dred and Harriet Scott and their daughters, Eliza and Lizzy, in their federal lawsuit for freedom.

The notoriety of Lovejoy's murder kept businesses and travelers away from Alton. The one-time jewel of the Mississippi stagnated and fell into decline. Leading citizens, including Krum, left in search of new opportunities, which some of them found in St. Louis.

But while the horrors of McIntosh's and Lovejoy's deaths impelled some people toward the idea of abolishing slavery, they had the opposite effect on others. Those deaths signaled the strength of the proslavery movement in Missouri, which only got stronger in the ensuing years. The legislature passed new laws stripping free African Americans of rights, and courts increasingly choked off the grounds upon which enslaved people could sue for freedom.

The *Missouri Republican* blamed McIntosh and Lovejoy for their own deaths.[94]

African Americans in St. Louis likely received a clear message: not even a white man could escape slavers' thugs by going across the border to Illinois.

6

SUING FOR FREEDOM AT THE CIRCUIT COURT

A new monument to the hundreds of enslaved people who sued for freedom in Missouri was unveiled in June 2022 at Market and Eleventh Streets.

A Missouri territorial statute from 1807 allowed a person held in bondage to sue for freedom. It was made part of Missouri state law in 1824. The person suing for freedom had to prove both that he or she was free and that he or she had been physically abused while being held as a slave.[95]

One way to prove you were free was to prove that you were descended in the maternal line from a free woman. Another way was to prove that you had been legally freed and then wrongfully enslaved again. A slave with emancipation papers and witnesses might prevail in such a case. Enslaved people often sued on the basis that they had lived for a time in a state where slavery was prohibited.

The Missouri Supreme Court adopted the principle "once free, always free" in 1824, ruling that an enslaved person became free if taken by a master into a state or territory where slavery was not allowed, and such freedom was permanent. Returning to a slave state did not strip it away.[96] The state's highest court retreated from that doctrine in the late 1840s, however. By 1852, it had become nearly impossible for an enslaved person to win a freedom suit in Missouri.

Between three hundred and four hundred slaves sued for freedom between 1812 and 1860.[97] Many of those who sued between 1824 and 1844 won their freedom. The significance of those suits as a route to freedom was probably

A monument to the hundreds of enslaved people in St. Louis who sued for their freedom in the circuit court was erected in June 2022. *Peter Downs.*

less than the numbers suggest, however, because different members of a family would file independent lawsuits.

Lucy Delaney was one person who won freedom from slavery via a freedom suit. She described her suit and her mother's in a book published in the 1890s.[98] Lucy's mother, Polly Crocket, was a free girl in Illinois when she and four other free African Americans were seized by slavers, bound and gagged, and taken across the Mississippi River to be sold into slavery in St. Louis. The flipside of the nearness of freedom for slaves on the west bank of the Mississippi in Missouri was the nearness of slavery for African Americans on the east bank of the Mississippi in Illinois.

Polly eventually was allowed to marry another slave, and the couple had two daughters, Nancy and Lucy. The slave master, Taylor Berry, specified in a will written before his death in a duel that they were to be freed after the death of his wife. The widow Berry's new husband did not follow those instructions, however. He was Robert Wash, a proslavery member of the Missouri Supreme Court from 1825 to 1837 who frequently dissented from decisions granting freedom to enslaved people who brought freedom suits. Wash kept the Crocket family enslaved after the widow Berry died and sold Polly's husband "way down South."

Polly aimed to find a way to get her and her girls to freedom. Opportunity came first for Nancy. Berry's daughter was going to Philadelphia to get married and wanted to take Nancy with her as a waiting maid. When the newlyweds stopped at Niagara Falls, hotel servants helped Nancy escape across the border to Canada.

Soon after Berry's daughter and her husband returned to St. Louis in 1837, they auctioned off Polly as punishment for talking back when she was ordered to do something. She escaped before they could hand her over to the buyer, however. Slave catchers caught up with her in Chicago. On being brought back to St. Louis, she somehow got hold of a lawyer and sued for her freedom.[99] The jury ruled that she was a free woman after several witnesses testified to her kidnapping. That left twelve-year-old Lucy alone in slavery.

Lucy ran to her mother's house in mid-1842 when threatened with being sold down the river for resisting a beating. Polly then hired Francis Murdoch, the former Alton city attorney, to file a freedom suit for Lucy. Her enslavers demanded that Lucy be locked in jail—the Sixth Street jail, the same jail in which Mary Meachum would later be locked up—pending trial. She remained in lockup for seventeen months until the trial was concluded. The prospect of being locked in jail while awaiting a hearing on your lawsuit, something your enslaver had the right to demand,[100] probably deterred some enslaved people from seeking their freedom through the court.

Lucy's trial lawyer was Edward Bates, who would later become Lincoln's attorney general. A jury ruled that she was free in February 1844 after hearing witnesses, including Robert Wash, testify that she was Polly's daughter. As the daughter of a free woman, she could not legally be a slave.

The most famous of St. Louis freedom suits was that of Dred and Harriet Scott, because that suit led in a direct path to the start of the Civil War.[101] Dred and Harriet Scott filed their suit in 1846, relying on the "once free, always free" principle and prior Missouri rulings that a slave taken to live in a state where slavery was illegal became free.

U.S. Army surgeon John Emerson took Dred Scott to Illinois, a free state, in 1832 and later took him to the Wisconsin Territory, where slavery

Memorial to Dred and Harriet Scott on the Fourth Street side of the Old Courthouse.
Peter Downs.

was banned by the Missouri Compromise. There Scott married Harriet Robinson, and her owner transferred her to Emerson. They all returned to St. Louis in 1842. Emerson died in 1843. Dred Scott tried several times to buy his freedom from Emerson's widow, Irene, but she refused. She made money off of Dred and Harriet by hiring them out to work for others.

Dred and Harriet Scott filed separate suits for freedom in April 1846, naming Irene Emerson as their enslaver. Their first attorney was Francis Murdoch, the same attorney who filed Lucy's petition for freedom.[102] Murdoch had an office at 10 South Fourth Street[103] (currently the site of the American Fur Exchange Building) kitty-corner from the federal courthouse. His office was just a couple of blocks from where Harriet is believed to have been living. His residence, on Seventh Street at the end of Elm Street,[104] was roughly five blocks from the African Baptist Church. Between 1844 and 1846, Murdoch filed more freedom suits in St. Louis than any other lawyer.[105]

At least one historian thinks Harriet was likely the driving personality behind the Scotts' suits for freedom.[106] The Meachums' church may have played a role in her decision. Harriett likely lived three blocks from the Meachums' church from 1844 to 1846 and probably attended the church.[107] It was the only African American church in St. Louis at the time. John Berry Meachum frowned on freedom suits—he was the defendant in three of them himself—but no one knows what Mary had to say about them. Mary, as the pastor's wife, likely would have been active in organizing the activities of women in the congregation. She probably developed the skills she displayed later in life—organizing escapes, refugee aid and care of wounded soldiers—while organizing women in the church.

Regardless of whether Mary or John Berry Meachum encouraged Harriet to sue, the church gave Harriet opportunities to talk to other Black women, free and enslaved, to get information about freedom and the law. Other women in the church had won freedom by filing suit, and Murdoch was bringing suits for several others.[108] She also would have met John Richard Anderson, who had returned to St. Louis after Lovejoy's murder and became a minister in the African Baptist Church.[109] Anderson was enslaved from infancy to Bates's sister Sarah but was freed when he was twelve. Historians disagree on whether it was Edward or Sarah who legally freed Anderson, but contemporaries attributed the responsibility for the act to Edward Bates.[110]

Since Anderson knew both Bates and Murdoch, two lawyers who represented enslaved people seeking freedom, some historians speculate that he actively supported the Scotts in moving ahead with their lawsuit.[111] Of

African Baptist ministers performed baptisms at Chouteau's at Eighth and Clark before it was drained in 1855. Photo by Thomas Easterly. *Missouri Historical Society.*

course, Bates probably also knew John Berry Meachum, as he was a leader in the colonization society that employed John Berry.

Harriet later joined the Second African Baptist Church organized by Anderson and twenty-two other people from Meachum's congregation, but she was not one of the founding members. The Second African Baptist Church was formally organized on March 22, 1846,[112] which is when the Scotts must have been preparing their lawsuit. Murdoch filed the Scotts' petitions for freedom with the circuit court on April 6, 1846.[113]

The Scott cases were assigned to Judge John Krum,[114] the former mayor of Alton. He moved to St. Louis in 1838 and became a judge of the circuit court in 1843.[115]

About the time Emerson's lawyer responded to the Scotts' claims, Emerson's father, Alexander Sanford, helped organized the "Committee of 100" to further limit the rights of free African Americans. The committee, led by John O'Fallon, who had been the foreman in the grand jury that declined to indict anyone for McIntosh's lynching, held large, raucous public

The Westin Hotel at Cupples Station occupies the former Chouteau's Pond site, where African Baptists used to hold baptisms. *Peter Downs*.

meetings in the rotunda of the federal courthouse at night. Sanford was a member of the governing committee.[116]

Within two weeks of the committee's first meeting, the sheriff began a campaign to arrest free Blacks who did not have a freedom license on them when they were stopped and questioned. Within a year, the state legislature had adopted the group's proposals to outlaw the teaching of reading or writing to African Americans and to restrict African American church services.[117]

Krum always seemed to have an ear turned to the demands of white mobs. When a riverboat worker challenged the requirement to always carry his freedom license, Krum ruled that free African Americans have no constitutional rights because they aren't citizens, and they can't be citizens because they aren't white.[118] The ruling presaged Chief Justice Roger Taney's opinion in the Dred Scott case. Krum later supported Senator Stephen A. Douglas's doctrine of (white) popular sovereignty. He was a Douglas delegate to the 1860 Democratic Convention that nominated Douglas for president and was chairman of the convention's credentials committee.[119]

By the time the Scotts' case came to trial at St. Louis Circuit Court on June 30, 1847, Krum no longer was a circuit court judge, and the Scotts were on their third lawyer. Murdoch had been driven out of town by former judge Bryan Mullanphy, who also was the city's tenth mayor.[120] Their second lawyer, Charles Drake, also left town. Drake had performed legal work for John Berry Meachum[121] and, by marriage to one of the Blow sisters, was related to the family bankrolling the Scotts' lawsuit. The Scotts' cases would last ten years and result in a U.S. Supreme Court ruling that no state could outlaw slavery.

Samuel Russell testified in the trial that he hired the Scotts from Irene Emerson and paid her father for them, but his testimony was ruled inadmissible after he admitted that his wife made the arrangements. The jury then ruled against the Scotts on the basis that there was no evidence that they were Emerson's slaves. The judge, however, encouraged them to refile.

The legal climate was changing, however. The Missouri Supreme Court was no longer the same court that had ruled that slaves taken to free states became free. It was intent on closing that door to freedom, and local courts followed its lead. In the two years after the St. Louis court freed Lucy Delaney, for example, only one of the twenty-five freedom suits that went to trial in St. Louis resulted in freedom for the plaintiff.[122]

The Scotts nevertheless filed suit again and won freedom after a second trial in 1850, with new witnesses testifying that Irene Emerson claimed to own them. Irene appealed to the Missouri Supreme Court. The Scotts probably had thought their lawsuit was routine. They may not have realized they were taking on the heart of the slave-owning aristocracy in St. Louis, the Chouteaus. The premier enslaving family in St. Louis got involved in the case through Irene's brother, who had married into the Chouteau family and rose to a position of leadership in their business affairs.

It appears the fix was in. Months before the Scotts' case reached the court, supreme court judges were talking among themselves and with select other attorneys about overturning the "once free, always free" doctrine as soon as they got a case that gave them the chance to do so.[123]

The Missouri Supreme Court overturned the trial decision for the Scotts and half a century of precedence in 1852 and ordered them enslaved once again. The two-to-one ruling rewrote state law by striking down the "once free, always free" doctrine and barred the door to future freedom suits.[124] The majority opinion held that slave status renewed when a slave returned to a slave state if he hadn't obtained freedom while in the free state or territory. The dissenting judge was Hamilton Gamble.

The Scotts did not have a lawyer when their case went to the Missouri Supreme Court. Their previous lawyer had died, and no one appeared on

City Hall sits on the site once occupied by Henri Chouteau's mansion. *Missouri Historical Society*.

their behalf at the court.[125] When the judgment reached the circuit court, however, the circuit judge declined to inscribe the supreme court's decision as the final judgment and instead stayed the ruling to give the Scotts time to appeal to the federal court.[126] He also may have suggested they contact his friend Roswell Field.[127]

7

THE ST. LOUIS CATHEDRAL AT THE GATEWAY ARCH NATIONAL PARK

About one hundred yards south of the new entrance to the Gateway Arch is the Old Cathedral, which was completed in 1834, a year and a half before the McIntosh atrocity. It was the seat of the Catholic bishop of St. Louis and the home parish for the Chouteau-led French Creole aristocracy.

The Chouteaus were the city's richest family. They had founded the European colony of St. Louis, once owned the whole county and underwrote the cost of building the cathedral.[128] They also were related to Irene Emerson by marriage.

Irene's brother John, who managed the defense against the Scotts' freedom lawsuits, had married Emilie Chouteau, the eldest child of Pierre Chouteau Jr., the undisputed head of the extended Chouteau family. John was devoted to the Chouteaus. He was determined to impress the old man and was treated like the eldest son in return.[129]

The Chouteaus determinedly and diligently defended what they perceived as their prerogative to enslave others. The extended family held over one hundred people in slavery in 1860. The people they enslaved included Native Americans as well as African Americans. They almost never freed anyone. They aggressively fought every lawsuit by an enslaved person seeking freedom, appealing every ruling that didn't go their way as high they could, in one case keeping the string of appeals going for fifteen years and trying, unsuccessfully, to get an appeal heard by the U.S. Supreme Court.[130] And they relentlessly pursued enslaved people who ran away.

Above: The old St. Louis Cathedral was the home parish for prominent slave-owning families in the nineteenth century. *Missouri Historical Society*.

Opposite: Today, the old St. Louis Cathedral is part of the Gateway Arch National Park. *Peter Downs*.

They got involved in the Scotts' case through John Sanford and may have subsidized Emerson's fight against the Scotts' freedom suit. The Chouteau family lawyers, former U.S. attorney general Reverdy Johnson and U.S. senator Henry Geyer, represented Sanford before the U.S. Supreme Court. Geyer had represented the State of Missouri in the lawsuit, in which Judge Krum ruled that African Americans had no constitutional rights.[131] Geyer successfully peddled the same argument to the U.S. Supreme Court.[132]

Among the cathedral's other parishioners were the Fuszes. Paul Fusz was arrested during the Civil War as a spy. He was caught with James Morgan Utz trying to smuggle a codebook, letters and information about St. Louis defenses to the Confederate army. They were disguised as Union soldiers. Utz was hanged shortly before a pardon arrived from President Lincoln.[133] Fusz's life was spared.

The cathedral, with its slave-owning parishioners, was for Elijah Lovejoy the physical symbol of a fusion of Catholicism and slavery. He launched diatribes against both while working almost in the shadow of the building until he was chased out of the city.

8

THE OLD FEDERAL COURTHOUSE

The old federal courthouse is where Roswell Field filed a federal lawsuit for the Scotts after the Missouri Supreme Court reversed the trial court decision freeing them. The Scotts filed their new lawsuit in 1853, this time also claiming freedom for their daughters. This time, the suit was against Irene's brother John Sanford, who claimed to own them.

It is not known if the Scotts ever entered the courthouse. It would have taken a lot of courage to do so. The courthouse formed the eastern side of institutions grouped around what is now Kiener Plaza that were at the heart of slavocracy in St. Louis. The courthouse hosted auctions of enslaved people at least once a week on the Fourth Street steps at noon, when nearly everyone in the city could see them.[134] One block to the west was the city jail, where the Scotts might have been locked up when they first filed suit for their freedom if Henry T. Blow and Joseph Charless had not stood bond for them. Across the street from the jail was the office of the slave traders Bolton, Dickens and Company. Another block due west was the site where McIntosh was lynched. On the south side of the rectangle was the mansion of Pierre Chouteau Jr., head of the slave-owning Chouteau clan.

The Scotts' federal lawsuit did not languish, as their state suit had. The U.S. Circuit Court ruled against them in 1854, a year before Mary Meachum was arrested for allegedly helping Esther try to escape from her enslavement to Henry Shaw. The Scotts appealed to the U.S. Supreme Court, and the court agreed to hear their case.

The old federal courthouse as it appeared in 1851. Photo by Thomas Easterly. *Missouri Historical Society.*

The Scotts needed a high-powered attorney to argue the case before the court. Field went to the politically powerful Blair brothers' law firm, whose office was less than a block from his at Third and Chestnut.[135] The younger brother, Frank, was the leader of the antislavery "free soil" movement in Missouri. The older brother, Montgomery, was then living in Washington, D.C. The family was among the elite of the Democratic Party. The father had been a close confidant of President Andrew Jackson.

Charlotte Blow Charless might have urged the Blairs to take the case. Dred Scott had been enslaved by Charlotte's widowed father and sold around the time of his death.[136] As the eldest surviving child, Charlotte took on the role of caretaker of her younger brothers and sisters. Her husband, Joseph Charless Jr., paid for the younger boys' education and brought them into his business. One historian argues that Charlotte was the driving force behind the Blows' and Charlesses' support for the Scotts.[137] It is unclear when Charlotte met Frank Blair, but she moved into his house after her husband's murder.[138]

Montgomery Blair agreed to represent the Scotts after the editor of a national antislavery magazine promised to cover the costs.[139]

The U.S. Supreme Court heard the Scotts' case in February 1857. The Scotts' cause had become celebrated across the North by that time. Their lawsuit embarrassed a leading abolitionist from Massachusetts, Congressman Calvin Chaffee. Chaffee had married Irene Emerson in 1850 without knowing about the Scott case, or so he claimed. Just weeks before the Supreme Court handed down its decision, newspapers reported that Chaffee was the owner through marriage of the celebrated Scotts! He was ridiculed and attacked in the press and by political opponents in the House of Representatives for arguing in Congress for the abolition of slavery while opposing freedom for his own slave in court.[140]

The Supreme Court ruled against the Scotts by a seven-to-two majority. Chief Justice Roger Taney wrote the sharply worded majority opinion and sought to end the nation's debate over slavery for all time with a resounding victory for slaveholders. No Black person could be a citizen of the United States, he wrote, and thus no Black person ever had standing to sue in a federal court.

Taney declared that the U.S. Constitution protected the rights of slavers to own slaves anywhere in the United States and concluded that the exclusion of slavery from the Northwest Territories in the Northwest Territorial Ordinance of 1789 and from certain states in the Missouri Compromise of

The old federal courthouse, where Dred and Harriet Scott sued for freedom, is part of the Gateway Arch National Park. *Peter Downs.*

Auctions of enslaved people were held on the eastern steps of the courthouse at least once a week before the Civil War. *Peter Downs*.

1820 was unconstitutional. Blacks, he wrote, were so far inferior to whites "that they had no rights which the white man was bound to respect."[141]

Northern Republicans assailed the decision as an assault on their states' right to ban slavery and to allow African American men to hold citizenship and vote. President James Buchanan followed the court's decision with the announcement that slavery was henceforth legal in all U.S. territories.

The decision must have devastated many African American antislavery activists who, like Mary Meachum, had spent decades working against slavery. It cut off all legal avenues to freedom with one blow, extended the reach of slavers to every part of the United States and, if embraced by the states, potentially stripped African Americans of all of the legal protections they used to carry on their struggle against slavery. The rights Meachum had relied on—including the right to worship as she pleased, the right to buy and free slaves and the right to a jury trial—could be swept away by the logic of the U.S. Supreme Court.

The champions of slavery were exuberant and pressed forward to stamp out what little shoots of African American freedom existed in Missouri. They dominated in races for the state general assembly in 1858 and, in 1860, overwhelmingly approved a bill to enslave all free African Americans between the ages of eighteen and fifty in the state. The governor vetoed the bill after the legislature adjourned.[142] There is no telling what the general assembly would have done in 1861 if the Civil War had not intervened.

Some abolitionists saw the ruling as an existential threat to the United States. In light of such incidents as Lovejoy's killing, it threatened the civil rights of white Americans to free speech, free press and freedom of religion and struck directly at the foundations of liberty. For Frank Blair, who had long painted slavery as a tool the rich used to oppress working people, Taney's ruling threatened opportunities for homesteading and farming across the country.

Abraham Lincoln said in his "House Divided" speech that if the ruling stood, "We shall lie down pleasantly dreaming that the people of Missouri are on the verge of making their State free; and we shall awake to the reality, instead, that the Supreme Court has made Illinois a slave State."[143]

"It does not stop with the negro," he said in debating Steven Douglas for a U.S. Senate seat in 1858, but also threatened the rights of German, Irish, French and Scandinavian immigrants, and of anyone who was not English.[144]

Lincoln's speeches after the Dred Scott decision vaulted him into the national limelight and on a path to the White House. The appearance of the Supreme Court trying to impose the will and practices of Southern slavers on the whole country paved the way to the Civil War.

For the Scotts, however, the decision ended on a personally happier note. Chaffee pressured Irene to sell the Scotts to someone who would free them. She sold them to Taylor Blow, but on the condition that she also receive all the wages they had earned for the previous seven years. Three months after the Supreme Court decision, the Scotts were free. Dred Scott died sixteen months later from tuberculosis.

9

FIELD HOUSE MUSEUM

Roswell Field, the Scotts' sixth lawyer, lived at what is now 634 South Broadway, about two blocks from the Meachums' church and six blocks from the courthouse. He may have walked by the African Baptist Church every day on his way to his office.

Field took the Scotts' case for free. His challenge was to figure out how to get it to the federal courts with a chance of winning. If he appealed the state supreme court's decision directly to the U.S. Supreme Court, the latter would likely follow its then standard practice of deferring to state law, which would leave the state court's decision in place. Another possibility was to sue someone in another state, as federal courts had jurisdiction over disputes between citizens of different states.[145]

John Sanford, who had claimed in Missouri court that he and not his sister owned the Scotts, had moved to New York when the Chouteau's American Fur Company opened an office there. Field made him the target of the lawsuit filed in federal court in November 1853 on behalf of "Dred Scott, of St. Louis, in the State of Missouri, and a citizen of the United States."

Despite Sanford's lawyer's claim that Scott was not a citizen because he was "a negro of African descent," U.S. District Judge Robert Wells ruled the federal court had jurisdiction to hear the case. Although the jury in the case ultimately ruled against Scott, the ruling on jurisdiction opened the way to the Supreme Court. Field, in his advice to Montgomery Blair, urged him to avoid the citizenship question and focus on American case law that said a slave transported to a free state by his master becomes forever free, because

Roswell Field's house was the last of a row of twelve houses built in the late 1840s. This is how they looked in 1910. *Missouri Historical Society.*

The Field House was saved from the wrecking ball to celebrate Roswell Field's son Eugene Field, who was famous for his children's poems and humorous essays. *Peter Downs.*

Right: The Dents' townhouse, which once stood at Fourth and Cerre behind and across the street from the Fields', hosted the wedding of Ulysses Grant and Julia Dent. *Missouri Historical Society*.

Below: Wealthy in-laws could boost the fortunes of young officers. General Winfield Scott Hancock's in-laws built for him this house, which once stood near Jefferson Barracks. Photo by Emil Boehl. *Missouri Historical Society*.

if the Supreme Court allowed the jurisdiction ruling to stand it would cut the ground out from under the Fugitive Slave Act.[146]

Field had been a proslavery Democrat as a young lawyer in Vermont, but the murders of Francis McIntosh and Elijah Lovejoy turned him against slavery and set him on the path that led to his representing Dred and Harriet Scot and their daughters Eliza and Lizzy. His law partner eventually drew up the Scotts' emancipation papers after Irene Emerson transferred ownership to Taylor Blow.[147]

Behind and across Cerre Street from the Field House was the house where Ulysses S Grant got married. Grant married Julia Dent on the night of August 22, 1848, in a simple, candlelit ceremony.[148] The then Captain Grant was stationed at Jefferson Barracks. His best man was James Longstreet, later a general in the Confederate army. The Dents maintained the townhouse in St. Louis in addition to their main residence on a plantation outside of town. Julia's father was vociferously proslavery.

There was nothing unusual about a society girl marrying an officer from the barracks. Indeed, there was a bit of a cottage industry in daughters from wealthy families marrying officers from the barracks. Other Civil War generals married to St. Louis gals included John Frémont (Republican candidate for president in 1856), John Harney, Andrew Jackson Smith and Winfield Scott Hancock (Democratic candidate for president in 1880).

10

LEGAL ROW

Roswell Field's and the Blairs' law offices were neighbors. Field's was on the north side of Chestnut Street between Second and Third Streets.[149] The Blairs' was on the southwest corner of Chestnut and Third.[150] It is an area now occupied by the Gateway Arch Park and the Park over the Highway.

The Blair brothers, Montgomery and Frank, had been making names for themselves in Missouri politics since moving to the state from Kentucky. Montgomery was appointed the U.S. district attorney for Missouri in 1839 and later served as mayor of St. Louis and judge of the common pleas court. Frank joined his brother in St. Louis in 1842, working first for Senator Thomas Hart Benton.

Frank and his cousin Benjamin Gratz Brown were elected to the Missouri House of Representatives in August 1852.[151] Gratz Brown had moved to Missouri to join the Blairs' law practice in 1849, then joined Frank Blair and William McKee in starting a Free-Soil newspaper, the *Missouri Democrat*, in July 1852.[152] Frank established a reputation for opposing politicians like Claiborne Jackson, who wanted to expand slavery to every territory of the United States. He called the expansion movement a plot to destroy the union and subvert the authority of Congress.[153]

Montgomery moved to Maryland in 1853 and established a law practice in Washington, D.C. He aspired to a seat on the U.S. Supreme Court.[154] For Field, that meant he was in place to argue a case before the court.

The Blairs were influential, but they also were somewhat odd allies for African Americans seeking freedom. As the Scott case began its path through the federal courts, the Blairs espoused Benton's middle-of-the-road policy of downplaying the issue of slavery and trying to reassure both pro- and antislavery voters. They told one side that slavery as an institution was safe and permanent where it existed and told the other side that the institution of slavery should not expand to where it did not already exist. Frank Blair undoubtedly approved of Brown's editorial of July 12, 1855, characterizing both abolitionists and secessionists as arsonists setting fire to opposite sides of the house at the same time.[155]

The Blairs and their cousin soon joined the new Republican Party, however. Frank won election to the U.S. House of Representatives in 1856 as a Free-Soil Democrat and then immediately switched parties to become the first Republican member of the U.S. House from a state where slavery was legal.[156] Brown won election again to the Missouri House of Representatives.

Frank won national attention with a proposal to marry the gradual abolition of slavery, with compensation for slave owners, to the deportation of African Americans to a yet-to-be-established U.S. colony in Central America.[157] He actively courted Lincoln to draw him to the side of colonization.[158] He urged Lincoln and Illinois Republicans to follow his lead and "drop the negro and go whole hog for the white man."[159] He was at least partially successful, as Lincoln emerged in 1858 as a prominent public voice for colonization and separation of the races.[160]

Frank had retooled his father's old racial argument against aristocratic abolitionists and turned it into an argument against slavocracy. Francis P. Blair Sr. had been an influential member of Andrew Jackson's "kitchen cabinet" and editor of the *Washington Globe*, the mouthpiece of Jackson's Democratic Party, for fifteen years. He campaigned against the Whig party, saying that Whigs embraced abolitionism as a means to degrade white workingmen and push them down to the level of the slaves.[161]

Frank Blair and Gratz Brown compared slave owners to the aristocracy from which so many German immigrants in St. Louis had fled. They said the existence of slavery deprived German and Irish immigrants of opportunities and forced free white laborers to compete with slaves for work. Many foreign-born workers in St. Louis were, in fact, doing jobs that had once been filled by enslaved people, and they could still see slaves working in some such jobs somewhere in the city.

The *Missouri Democrat* kicked off a campaign for a "Free White Labor Movement" in 1858 with the slogan "White Men for Missouri, Missouri for White Men."[162] Frank Blair and the *Democrat* energetically campaigned for

Lincoln in southern Illinois in the Senate election of 1858, and Blair stayed in close contact with Lincoln thereafter.

The Blair family was determined to prevent the "radicals" from taking over the Republican Party in 1860 and nominating William Seward for president. They convinced Edward Bates to run for the nomination[163] but were prepared to back Abraham Lincoln as their second choice.

11

EDWARD BATES AND GRAPE HILL

Edward Bates was probably the St. Louis politician with the greatest national prominence after the death of Thomas Hart Benton. He lived on his Grape Hill estate east of Euclid on what is now called Duncan Avenue from 1851 until he moved to Washington, D.C., in 1861 to serve as Abraham Lincoln's attorney general. He sold the property after returning to St. Louis in 1864. The homesite now is occupied by a parking garage for the BJC Center for Advanced Medicine.

Bates had moved to St. Louis as a young man after President Thomas Jefferson appointed his older brother secretary of the new Missouri Territory. Edward Bates helped draft the first constitution for the State of Missouri in 1820. His brother was elected as the state's second governor.

Bates was a judicial conservative who opposed the expansion of slavery. He joined the Colonization Society in the 1820s and later joined Elijah Lovejoy and Joseph Charless in a group that advocated the gradual emancipation of enslaved people.[164] He became president of the state colonization society in 1850.[165] He probably knew John Berry Meachum as one of the society's agents.

Nonetheless, Bates had long enslaved others when he undertook to represent Polly Crocket's daughter Lucy in a freedom suit. Polly was born free but kidnapped and enslaved. When she had children, they were enslaved as well. Their cases may have influenced Bates's views on slavery. He began a continuous process of freeing people he had enslaved in the same year that Lucy won her freedom. By 1851, he and his wife had transitioned his

Edward Bates, a prominent antislavery politician in Missouri, served as Abraham Lincoln's attorney general. This statue is in Forest Park. *Peter Downs*.

household to no longer rely on slave labor and he freed his last slave. During that transition, he and his family lived in a two-story house on the northwest corner of Sixteenth Street and Chestnut. City View Apartments now occupies the site. Bates had lived at Sixth and Market during Polly's trial.

Bates's political career was built largely around opposition to Thomas Hart Benton and Jacksonian Democrats, although he joined with Benton in opposing the war on Mexico.[166] It included terms in the Missouri and U.S. Houses of Representatives. He had hoped for a cabinet position with President Zachary Taylor but turned down the position of secretary of war in President Millard Fillmore's cabinet. He presided over the Whig Convention in 1856, when delegates representing the remaining rump of the Whig Party endorsed the candidates of the American National Party (better known as the Know Nothing Party) for president and vice president.

The Blairs enticed him into running for the Republican Party nomination for president in 1860, although he hadn't joined the Republican Party. They believed he was just the person to unite former Whigs, antislavery Democrats and liberal former Know Nothings in a winning coalition for an election victory. They saw him as a potential bulwark against both radical abolitionists in the North and slavery expansionists in the South.[167]

Bates was considered the most conservative candidate in the Republican nomination race in 1860, but he was opposed not just by radical abolitionists but also by German Americans, an important part of the party base, because of his support for the anti-immigrant policies of the Know Nothings in 1856.[168] Many delegates initially pledged to Bates jumped on the Lincoln bandwagon when support for Bates failed to grow at the convention.

Bates came in fourth on the first ballot for the presidential nomination at the 1860 Republican Convention, behind William Seward, Abraham Lincoln and Salmon Chase. He and Chase both lost votes on the second ballot as delegates switched to one of the two front-runners, but mostly to Lincoln. After Lincoln secured a majority on the third ballot, the rest of the delegates switched their votes to Lincoln to make it unanimous.[169]

Bates accepted Lincoln's invitation to join his cabinet as attorney general. Lincoln rewarded the Blairs, too, giving Montgomery the position of postmaster general, which allowed him control of the largest patronage network in the government.

PART II

WAR BEGINS

Frank Blair and the Contest for Missouri

12

FRANK BLAIR JR.

William T. Sherman said that Frank Blair did "more than any single man" to keep St. Louis in the Union.[170] The center of his work was his home on the northeast corner of Twelfth Street (now called Tucker Boulevard) and Washington Avenue.

Between the election and Lincoln's inauguration, a period of four months in 1861, Frank organized on two levels to keep Missouri in the Union: political and military.

On the political level, Frank and other leading Republicans responded to Lieutenant Governor Thomas Reynolds's effort to rally the public in the city to support secession, and the formation of the secessionist Minute Men militia in early January,[171] with a rally of their own pledging unconditional support for the Union.[172]

After Unionist Democrats, including Bates's brother-in-law and law partner Hamilton Gamble, called a large meeting that supported maintaining the Union as long as the federal government recognized the "constitutional right" to own slaves and condemned the seizure of federal property by states, Blair saw an opening for a political coalition against secession.[173]

With the state legislature calling for a state convention to consider secession, Blair and the Republican leadership reached out to Unionist Democrats to select a broad Union slate for the elections. They met at the Mercantile Library on January 31 and hammered out a deal. They went on to a dominant win in the elections to the special state convention. No one

Frank Blair is celebrated with a statue in Forest Park near the intersection of Kingshighway and Lindell. *Peter Downs*.

who ran as an outright secessionist won election to the meeting, and genuine Unionists won enough seats to prevent a secession bill from passing.[174]

On the military level, Frank was a leading figure in setting up the St. Louis Committee of Safety to equip a paramilitary force to fight secessionists. The committee consisted, along with Frank, of Mayer Giles Filley, Bates's former protégé James Broadhead, Samuel Glover, John Horn and Julius Witzig.[175] Witzig was a key link to leaders of the German community, who had begun arming and training well before Blair instigated the formation of a Committee of Safety. The German Turner Society, for example, had set up a rifle section shortly after incorporating in 1855. Franz Sigel was teaching tactics to the rifle section in February 1860, eleven months before the formation of the Committee of Safety, and in November 1860 military drill was incorporated into the gymnastic exercises required of all Turner Society members.[176]

The Turner Society let the Committee of Safety meet in the Turner Hall on Tenth Street (between Walnut and Market Streets) every night.[177] The Turner Hall was about a block from the new homes Mary Meachum had constructed in 1855 for herself and her son John,[178] now the site of the Eagleton Federal Courthouse.

A park at Tenth and Market marks the former site of the Turner Hall, which served as headquarters for the Unionist Committee of Safety. *Peter Downs*.

The Committee of Safety brought coordination to the militia efforts of Germans and others, creating the Home Guards and later answering Lincoln's call for volunteers. Initial recruitment efforts for the Home Guards targeted the ranks of the Wide Awakes (formed during the 1860 election to provide security at Republican campaign events against opponents intent on disrupting such events[179]), and German gun clubs and Turner clubs (turnvereins). They bought all the Sharpe's rifles available at Woodward's Hardware Store on Main Street and armed about fifty workers at Filley's stove factory. They got two hundred muskets from the Republican governor of Illinois and moved them to the Turner Hall for German Home Guards in empty beer barrels hidden within a beer delivery.[180]

Blair tapped Franz Sigel, one of the most popular leaders of the German community in St. Louis, to oversee drilling of Home Guard units. He lobbied his brother and Lincoln behind the scenes to get officers sympathetic to secession removed from positions of authority over the federal arsenal in St. Louis and offered his support to the new commander of troops guarding the arsenal when he arrived in February.[181]

13

BERTHOLD MANSION

The Berthold Mansion, on the site at Broadway and Pine now occupied by One Metropolitan Square, was the St. Louis headquarters for the Democratic Party in 1860 and the headquarters for the Missouri Minute Men in 1861 when the Minute Men tried to provoke a battle to justify secession.[182] The mansion had been built by Pierre Chouteau Jr.'s brother-in-law and business partner.

Basil Duke, chairman of the Military Committee of the Minute Men, wrote in his *Reminiscences* that there were about four hundred men in the Minute Men, organized into five companies. "We wished to enlist only the kind of material which could be relied on for any service and in any emergency, and no more than we could arm."[183] General Daniel Frost, commander of the Missouri Volunteer Militia, had extended the cloak of legitimacy to them three weeks earlier when he mustered them into the Volunteer Militia as a battalion under Colonel John S. Bowen's command and gave Duke the rank of captain.[184]

The Minute Men sought to influence the vote in a special state convention on secession that was due to meet two blocks from the Berthold Mansion at the Mercantile Library in St. Louis on March 4. They also sought to "incite a popular outbreak" that would provide cover and opportunity for a raid on the St. Louis arsenal. And they hoped to do these "without becoming ourselves the aggressors," Duke wrote.[185]

Duke was in charge of the Berthold Mansion headquarters, which was one block from the federal courthouse. He called the company commanders together on the night of March 3.

BERTHOLD MANSION, N. W. COR. BROADWAY AND PINE ST.

MRS. W. L. EWING, MRS. WILLIAM WAGGAMAN, MISS TULIA BERTHOLD. (Standing on porch).
MRS. BARTHOLOMEW BERTHOLD, MRS. SYLVESTRE LABADIE, MR. AMEDÉE BERTHOLD. (Sitting on porch).
CLAIRE KENNEDY, MAJ. WAGGAMAN. (On steps).

The Berthold Mansion on Broadway near Pine was the headquarters of the secessionist Minute Men militia. *Missouri Historical Society.*

"[W]e decided to display on the succeeding day such unmistakable symbols of secession and evidence of an actively rebellious disposition as would be a plain defiance to the Union sentiment and challenge to the Wide Awakes," he wrote.[186]

Duke wrote as if he thought that the majority of convention delegates were Southern sympathizers who were just too timid to voice their convictions—the "silent majority" in modern political rhetoric. What they needed, the Minute Men commanders thought, was a demonstration to stiffen their resolve. They thought flying two secession flags might do it. One they hung from the summit of the courthouse dome. The other they hung from the front porch of the mansion.

Duke summoned about sixty of the "most determined and reckless" Minute Men, as he described them,[187] put muskets and revolvers in their hands and stationed them around the mansion to protect the secessionist

The Metropolitan Square building stands on the former site of the Berthold Mansion.
Peter Downs.

flag. He positioned a small swivel cannon, primed and loaded with musket balls and nails, to blast anyone who broke through the mansion door.

Early in the morning, the flag on the courthouse was removed and a large, angry crowd gathered in front of the Berthold Mansion. Duke received reports that the Wide Awakes were forming up and noted the loudness of their drumming. He and his men waited anxiously for an attack.

"While unwilling to fire on the mob without the amplest provocation, we were determined to fire on the Wide Awakes so soon as they were in sight," he wrote.[188]

But instead of Blair's Wide Awakes, the police and the state militia arrived, the latter under the command of General Daniel Frost. It was a stalemate. Frost argued against making any concessions to the crowd protesting the secessionist flag and urged Mayor Filley to turn the police and fire hoses on the crowd. The mayor refused to do so.

"The opportunity we had hoped and striven for did not occur," Duke wrote.[189]

Blair and his commanders surely realized the convention was a bigger prize than a flag on the Berthold Mansion porch. They were not diverted by Duke's provocation and did not fall into his trap.

Three weeks later, the Confederate-leaning state legislature stripped the Republican mayor of control of the police and put the department under the command of a four-person Board of Police Commissioners consisting of Duke and three other secessionists. Duke lamented that it was too late to affect the political situation.[190]

(A year later, General John Schofield was using the Berthold Mansion as a regimental hospital for a new Unionist Missouri State Guard.[191])

MERCANTILE LIBRARY

The Mercantile Library at 510 Locust Street was the site of the 1861 convention that Duke tried to influence. It was only two blocks from the Berthold Mansion, where Duke raised the flag of secession. It later housed the 1865 convention that abolished slavery in Missouri.

The state's newly elected governor, Claiborne Jackson, was a staunch advocate of slavery. He had sponsored a set of resolutions in the state general assembly in 1848 that directed Missouri's senators to support the doctrines of South Carolina senator John Calhoun, which claimed the federal government had no power to prevent slave owners from migrating to any U.S. territory with their "property." Judge William Napton of the Missouri Supreme Court drafted the resolutions for Jackson and intended to apply Calhoun's doctrines to the Dred and Harriet Scott case when it reached his court.[192]

Jackson ran for governor in 1860 as a Unionist Democrat and supporter of Stephen Douglas, however, in order to get elected. Once in power, he sided with secessionists at the first opportunity.[193] He reacted to South Carolina's secession from the United States by asking the state assembly to call for a state convention to vote on secession for Missouri. The legislature accordingly passed a bill on January 18, 1861, for elections to such a convention.

Jackson likely felt confident of success, as Lincoln had garnered only 17,000 of the 165,500 votes cast for president in Missouri. But this is where Frank Blair's political skills shined. Not one avowed secessionist won election to the convention.

The Mercantile Library hosted the special state convention to consider secession in 1861 and the convention that abolished slavery in 1865. Photo by Richard Henry Fuhrmann. *Missouri Historical Society*.

The convention met first in Jefferson City on February 28 before convening in St. Louis on March 4. Hamilton Gamble, Bates's brother-in-law, law partner and political ally, dominated the proceedings. As chairman of the Federal Relations Committee, he reported out resolutions against secession and urged avoiding conflict.[194] The first resolution approved by the convention stated, "[T]here exists no adequate cause why Missouri should secede from the Union."

It also stated that the constitutional union was permanent, that the U.S. Constitution was the "supreme law of the land and not a mere compact" and that there was no provision for states to leave the Union legally.

The fifth resolution urged both sides "to withhold and stay the arm of military power, and on no pretense whatever bring upon the nation the horrors of civil war."[195]

A new Mercantile Library building was erected on the site of the old one in the mid-twentieth century. It is being converted into apartments. *Peter Downs*.

Thus, Missouri became the only state where a convention called to consider secession rejected it.[196] The convention met again in July 1861 after Jackson and other secessionists in state government fled before General Nathaniel Lyon's march on Jefferson City. The convention declared the executive offices vacant and appointed a provisional government, with Gamble as governor.

Jackson died of cancer not long after on December 6, 1862, in a rooming house near Little Rock.

SOULARD

S oulard was the center of German resistance to slavery and home to significant paramilitary support for the Union. The Second Regiment, Home Guards (later the Second Regiment, U.S. Army Reserve Corps) made Soulard Market its headquarters and armory.[197] The headquarters of the First Regiment was at Jaeger's Garden on the east side of South Tenth Street between Victor and Sidney.[198] The site now is part of a Girls' and Boys' Club. Students from the German Humboldt Institute drilled at Dr. Adam Hammer's house on the site now occupied by the Anheuser-Busch brewery.[199]

Robert and Roderick Rombauer, together with Anselm Albert, began the organization that would become the First Regiment.[200] The three were veterans of the failed 1848 liberal revolution in Hungary. They were convinced by January 1861 of the need to organize a military body to protect their neighborhoods from secessionists. They agreed to talk up the concept with other friends and at public gatherings.

Soon they had fourteen men willing to drill at Flora Garden on the west side of Seventh Street between Lafayette Avenue and Geyer. They had fifty men participating in drills by February 8. They also met in committees to decide how to grow and organize the group. They established a seven-member executive committee, which included Robert Rombauer, and divided the ward into eight districts. The First Ward covered everything from the city's southern boundary at Keokuk Street north to Soulard Street between the riverfront on the east and Jefferson Avenue on the west.

Jaeger's Garden was the headquarters for the First Regiment, Home Guards. This photo was taken by Robert Bennecke in 1870. *Missouri Historical Society.*

The Jaeger's Garden site is now an athletic field for Gene Slay's Girls & Boys Club. *Peter Downs.*

An organizing committee was appointed for each district to recruit new members and establish a district meeting place with the goal of bringing the ward guard up to 800 members by April 27. They exceeded the goal and enrolled 1,200 members. Of the total, 94 percent were immigrants from a German state; the other 6 percent were from Bohemia.[201] They were required to furnish their own equipment and food when on duty and assemble on short notice when needed.

Once enrolled into companies of one hundred men each, the men elected their officers. The companies were organized into two battalions and the battalions into a regiment. Henry Almstedt was elected colonel and commander of the regiment. Robert Rombauer was elected lieutenant colonel and second in command. He was in charge of the First Battalion and of tactical training.

Some of the men may have known Ulysses Grant. He had lived at two places in the ward in the late 1850s, first at the southwest corner of Lynch and Seventh Streets (now a parking lot for the Anheuser-Busch brewery), a couple of blocks from Dr. Hammer's house, and then at 1068 Barton Street. What they thought about him or the fact that he had slaves in his house is unknown.

The Second Regiment recruited from residents of the city's Second Ward, which stretched roughly from the riverfront to Jefferson Avenue between Soulard Street and Chouteau Avenue. The Second Regiment had nearly eight hundred men, 92 percent originally from a German state and 8 percent from Bohemia.[202]

These men lived near two men who likely embodied the slavocracy they opposed. Just north of Chouteau Avenue on Eighth Street, an outspoken advocate of slavery named Dr. Joseph McDowell threatened to bombard his German neighbors with the cannon he had installed at his medical college if they tried to enter the grounds of his college.[203]

Thomas Allen controlled the land on the western edge of the increasingly crowded Soulard neighborhood (the parallel east–west streets Ann, Russell and Allen were named for his wife, the former Ann Russell). Many Germans probably rented from him, some because they lived in his apartments, some because they built on land he or his wife owned. His real estate holdings were valued at $500,000 in the 1860 census, equivalent to nearly $17 million in 2020.

Allen, who lived on the west side of what is now Eighth Street between Ann and Russell, also enslaved people. There is no record of him emancipating any enslaved people before the Civil War, but there are records of him

$200 Reward.

RANAWAY from the subscriber, on the night of Thursday, the 30th of Sepember,

FIVE NEGRO SLAVES,

To-wit : one Negro man, his wife, and three children.

The man is a black negro, full height, very erect, his face a little thin. He is about forty years of age, and calls himself *Washington Reed*, and is known by the name of Washington. He is probably well dressed, possibly takes with him an ivory headed cane, and is of good address. Several of his teeth are gone.

Mary, his wife, is about thirty years of age, a bright mulatto woman, and quite stout and strong.

The oldest of the children is a boy, of the name of FIELDING, twelve years of age, a dark mulatto, with heavy eyelids. He probably wore a new cloth cap.

MATILDA, the second child, is a girl, six years of age, rather a dark mulatto, but a bright and smart looking child.

MALCOLM, the youngest, is a boy, four years old, a lighter mulatto than the last, and about equally as bright. He probably also wore a cloth cap. If examined, he will be found to have a swelling at the navel.

Washington and Mary have lived at or near St. Louis, with the subscriber, for about 15 years.

It is supposed that they are making their way to Chicago, and that a white man accompanies them, that they will travel chiefly at night, and most probably in a covered wagon.

A reward of $150 will be paid for their apprehension, so that I can get them, if taken within one hundred miles of St. Louis, and $200 if taken beyond that, and secured so that I can get them, and other reasonable additional charges, if delivered to the subscriber, or to THOMAS ALLEN, Esq., at St. Louis, Mo. The above negroes, for the last few years, have been in possession of Thomas Allen, Esq., of St. Louis.

WM. RUSSELL.

ST. LOUIS, Oct. 1, 1847,

Above: William Russell offered a reward for the capture and return of an enslaved family that had escaped from his son-in-law Thomas Allen. *Missouri Historical Society*.

Opposite: Soulard Market, the headquarters of the Second Regiment of Home Guards, was the scene of a battle with an American Party mob in 1852. This building replaced one destroyed by a tornado in 1896. *Peter Downs*.

offering rewards for the capture and return of enslaved people who ran away from him. On the surface, he fit the image that Blair, Brown and the *Missouri Democrat* tried to paint of a slave-owning American aristocrat, and some of the Germans in the neighborhood probably saw him that way. He supported the Union, however.

Soulard Market Hall, which the Second Regiment made its headquarters and armory, held a special meaning for the Germans. It had been the polling place for the First Ward in the 1852 election when it was seized by a mob from the American (Know Nothing) Party. The mob attacked voters, smashed open the ballot boxes and destroyed ballots and then attacked nearby German businesses. But Germans in the neighborhood recovered and counterattacked. A fire company arrived and turned its hoses on the

Germans and set fire to one of their buildings. The Germans, however, gained the upper hand and forced the anti-immigrant mob back.[204]

That attack delivered an important lesson in self-defense. Henry (Heinrich) Boernstein, editor of the *Anzeiger Des Westens*, which was among the businesses attacked during the riot, recruited and commanded a regiment of St. Louis Volunteers in 1861.[205]

16

THE FEDERAL ARSENAL

The St. Louis Arsenal at Second and Arsenal Streets contained the largest store of weapons of any slaveholding state in 1861: sixty thousand muskets, ninety thousand pounds of gunpowder, over one million cartridges, forty cannons and all the machinery necessary to make and repair guns.[206] That number of muskets was equal to 40 percent of all the muskets in states that seceded from the Union.

It was the object of intrigue within both the secessionist and Union camps in the first four months of 1861. Secessionists dreamed of what they could do with the arms stored there. Federalists had nightmares about it. Duke called the capture of the arsenal a "vital and immediate necessity" for the Confederacy in Missouri. He claimed: "An almost invincible force could have been promptly armed from this source, and such a force would have been at once recruited; for with the capture of the arsenal by the secessionists all doubt and vacillation would have disappeared from their ranks. It would have assured the most timid and hesitant, and have been the signal for an instant and overwhelming uprising, both in St. Louis and the state, on behalf of the Southern cause."[207]

Secessionists in Missouri had reason to think the weapons would go to them. Nineteen days after Lincoln won the vote for president in November 1860, Secretary of War John Floyd of the outgoing Buchanan administration instructed Major William Bell, the commander of the arsenal, to give General Frost whatever ammunition he wanted "under a requisition of the Govt. of Missouri."[208]

The federal arsenal was the focus of Unionist and Secessionist schemes in early 1861. This photo was taken by George Stark in 1905. *Missouri Historical Society.*

(Unionists would later accuse Floyd of treason. He had transferred 115,000 muskets and rifles from Northern arsenals to arsenals in Southern states in late 1859 and, in his last days in office, had tried to send heavy guns to Gulf Coast forts in Texas and Mississippi. President Buchanan personally revoked the orders shipping the heavy guns. Floyd was implicated in corrupt payment schemes with War Department contractors and compelled to resign at the end of December 1860.)

It was not as if Bell had the means to fight off an assault if he wanted to. The thirty-seven-acre, twenty-five-building arsenal complex was surrounded by a ten-foot-high stone wall but protected by a single guard. It appears, however, that Bell didn't want to fight anyway. General Daniel Frost, commander of the Missouri Volunteer Militia, reported to Governor Jackson on January 24 that Bell agreed that the weapons at the arsenal should be used to arm the state's secessionist militia. "The Major is with us," Frost reported. "He is everything that you and I could desire."[209] He even was willing to let the state militia send in troops to "guard" the munitions.

Bell's hold over the arsenal was coming to an end, however. General-in-Chief Winfield Scott dispatched forty soldiers to St. Louis on January 11 to guard the arsenal and the subtreasury, which was housed in the post office

Pigs of lead, used to make bullets, stacked on the west side of the arsenal's main building in 1862. *Missouri Historical Society*.

building downtown. The soldiers' commander, Lieutenant W.J. Robinson, was a St. Louisan and a Union man. He quietly contacted Frank Blair, who put him in touch with two of the German militia groups.[210] One of them, the Schwarze Jaeger (or Black Rifles), was a hunting and rifle club founded by former European soldiers. They began holding drills in front of the arsenal at what is now Lyons Park at Broadway and Arsenal. The location was new, but the practice wasn't. They had been meeting since at least 1852 for gun and rifle practice, hunting and social gatherings.[211]

General Daniel Frost, commander of the state militia, hatched a plan to circumvent the small contingent of federal troops and place his militia in the arsenal. He sent instructions to his subordinates to rally their forces upon the continuous pealing of church bells interrupted by a pause of five minutes and march to the arsenal to "protect it from mobs." Someone passed a copy of the order to Blair, who took it to Archbishop Peter Kenrick, who forbade priests in the diocese from taking part in the plot.[212]

Blair asked Bell for permission to send Home Guards to defend the arsenal, but Bell rejected the offer. Blair then sent a copy of Frost's circular

Cannon on east, or river-facing, side of the main arsenal building in an 1866 photo by Emil Boehl. *Missouri Historical Society*.

and an account of Bell's actions to his brother, President-Elect Lincoln and General Scott, commanding general of the U.S. Army, and lobbied for Bell's transfer.

Scott replaced Bell and put Brevet Major Peter Hagner in command.[213] He also reinforced Robinson with two more companies of regular troops. Captain Nathaniel Lyon, who arrived with the second company, was put in command of the troops guarding the arsenal. Scott quietly ordered more reinforcements in batches of one hundred or two hundred. By mid-February, Lyon had nearly five hundred soldiers serving under him.[214]

Hagner and Lyon often clashed, however. Some of the newly arrived officers had been evacuated from other arsenals seized by secessionists, such as at Baton Rouge and Little Rock. They were not pleased by what they saw as Hagner's interference in defensive preparations and tended to side with Lyon.[215] Lyon tried to circumvent Hagner by working closely with Frank Blair and Franz Sigel to bolster the defenses of the arsenal with armed civilians.[216]

Meanwhile, Jackson hoped for a legal basis for secession from the special state convention. When the convention failed to give him the legal cover he wanted, he moved toward secession anyway. Among the steps he took was to appoint Duke to the new St. Louis police board. Duke proposed, or had proposed in his name, the creation of a body of "special police" to act as "secret police" to gather information on Unionist organizing and arming. He recommended putting police captain Rock Champion in charge of the unit. Champion was one of the first members of Duke's Minute Men.[217] The board adopted Duke's plan and also gave police officers authority to stop anyone on the street who aroused suspicion and arrest them if they were not satisfied with their answers. They also adopted a plan to recruit two companies per ward to "suppress mobs or riots."[218]

The new mayor, a secessionist, also ordered beer gardens and halls, theaters and restaurants to close on Sundays. All were places where German Unionist clubs tended to meet.[219]

With hopes for a peaceful handover of the arsenal dashed, Governor Jackson decided to take the arsenal by force. He directed Duke and Cotton Greene in early April to go to Alabama to get heavy guns from CSA president Jefferson Davis and told Frost to collect a force on the outskirts of St. Louis to prepare to put the arsenal under siege. Meanwhile, he continued to assure General William Harney, the general in command of the Western District, which included Missouri, of his neutrality. Harney continued to try to block Lyon for fear of inflaming a tense situation.[220]

Lyon expected Frost to occupy the high ground west of the arsenal and bombard Union forces defending the arsenal.[221] Frost thought that was a good plan, too, and expected that it would force the Federal troops to surrender.[222]

Harney also thought that would happen and wrote to General Scott about it on April 16[223] but still tried to thwart Lyon's plans for defending the complex. When the War Department authorized Lyon to draw five thousand guns from the arsenal to arm the Home Guards, Harney told Lyon not to issue any arms without his consent. The St. Louis Police Board protested when Lyon sent troops to take control of the high ground above the arsenal, and Harney ordered Lyon to pull his men back within the arsenal walls. Harney even refused to let Lieutenant John Schofield muster volunteers into the Federal army after Schofield was detailed to do so by the War Department.[224]

After the Missouri Volunteer Militia captured the smaller federal arsenal in Liberty, Missouri, seizing the one thousand muskets, four cannons and the ammunition stored there,[225] Blair worked his political connections to support Lyon. Secretary of War Simon Cameron instructed Harney on April 21 to begin mustering volunteers. Events then began to move more quickly. The

This nineteenth-century memorial to Nathaniel Lyon stands in Lyon Park in front of the arsenal that he protected for the United States. *Peter Downs*.

next day, Governor Jackson ordered the mustering of the Missouri Volunteer Militia. The day after that, Cameron recalled Harney to Washington.

Duke and Cotton Greene traveled south as Jackson's emissaries to meet with Davis in Montgomery. They obtained an order for the commandant

Today, the arsenal serves as a U.S. geospatial intelligence center. *Peter Downs*.

of the Southern arsenal in Baton Rouge to give them two twelve-pound howitzers, two thirty-two-pound siege guns, five hundred muskets and a quantity of ammunition. Once in Baton Rouge, Duke and Greene chartered the steamboat *Swan* to smuggle the munitions upriver past Federal inspectors in Cairo.[226]

With Harney out of the way in St. Louis, Lyon completed enrollment in the volunteer regiments authorized by the War Department. The First Regiment was organized and led by Frank Blair; the Second by Henry Boernstein; the Third by Franz Sigel; and the Fourth, composed mostly of Schwarze Jaeger, by Nicolas Schuettner. Another regiment was organized a couple of weeks later under Charles Salomon after Lincoln increased Missouri's quota.[227] The leaders of all the regiments were given the rank of colonel.

Lyon also sent troops to reoccupy the heights above the arsenal, positioned riflemen in several rented buildings near the arsenal and, in a secret nighttime operation, moved twenty-one thousand muskets to a safer location in Alton, Illinois.

Lyon received an order on April 30, signed by Cameron, Scott and Lincoln, instructing him to work with the Committee of Safety to enroll an additional "Reserve Corps" of 10,000 men.[228] The First and Second

Uhrig's Cave served as the headquarters and armory for the Fourth Regiment of U.S. Reserve Corps, led by Benjamin Gratz Brown. *Missouri Historical Society.*

Ward militias instigated by the Rombauers formed the First and Second Regiments of the Reserve Corps. The Third Regiment, under John McNeil, was based at the Turner Hall and recruited from the area between Chouteau and Market. The Fourth Regiment recruited, under Blair's cousin B. Gratz Brown, was headquartered at Uhrig's Cave on the southwest corner of Washington and Jefferson Avenues. Brown recruited from the area around Franklin Avenue. Brewer Charles Stifel was organizing a fifth regiment in North St. Louis. The headquarters of Stifel's regiment was at his brewery at Eighteenth and Howard Streets.[229]

When Duke and Greene returned to St. Louis with arms from the Confederacy on May 9, Lyon had the forces at his disposal to do something about it.

17

CAMP JACKSON / ST. LOUIS UNIVERSITY CAMPUS

C amp Jackson" was the name the Missouri Volunteer Militia gave to the Lindell's Grove area, southeast of the present intersection of Grand Avenue and Lindell Boulevard. The militia's headquarters was between present-day Olive Street and Lindell Boulevard near North Theresa Avenue.

Militia volunteers gathered at Camp Jackson on May 6. It wasn't General Frost's first choice for a camp, but that had been denied them a week earlier when Lyon stationed troops and artillery on the high ground near the St. Louis Arsenal.[230] An estimated one thousand men or more marched and drilled and waited for the expected cannon and other weapons from the Confederacy.

Duke and the *Swan* reached St. Louis on the morning of May 9. The weaponry was packed in boxes labeled as marble.[231] Whatever Duke may have wished, there was no way to move cannon, rifles and ammunition from the river docks to Camp Jackson in broad daylight in secret, but Duke may not have been too concerned about it. The arrival of the guns was meant to bolster the confidence and fighting spirit of the Missouri Volunteers and their supporters. If word leaked out, so much the better.

Captain Lyon, commander of the St. Louis Arsenal, heard about it from dockhands.[232] He rode out to Camp Jackson disguised, according to one source, as an old blind woman in a black dress, bonnet and veil to check it out.[233] He met that evening with the Committee of Safety to report on the situation at Camp Jackson and discuss his plans to do something about it.

Soldiers at Camp Jackson in 1861. Photo by Murillo Studio. *Missouri Historical Society.*

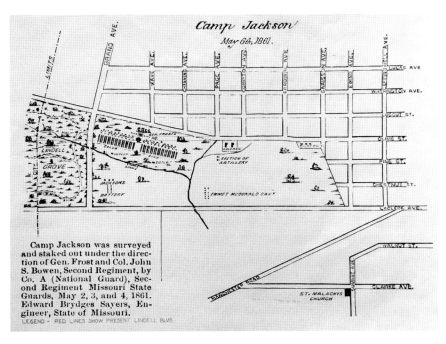

The layout of Camp Jackson, with troops concentrated near Olive Street east of Grand. *Missouri Historical Society.*

Blair was solidly behind Lyon's plan, but some other committee members preferred taking legal action through the courts.[234] At the same time, the chief of police met with the police board and reported that he thought an attack on Camp Jackson was imminent. Duke rode out to the camp and warned Frost to prepare for an attack in the morning.[235] Duke then hurried to report to Governor Jackson and urge him to tell Frost to either go on the offensive or retreat to a more defensible place.[236]

At least some of Frost's men were confident of victory. G.W. wrote to his brother on May 9 that Frost had about 1,800 men at Camp Jackson and more were joining every day. "[I]n a short time we shall have enough to bring the Union men or black Republicans into our terms, or force them to leave the State," he wrote. "I have just received news that Capt. Lyon intends to attack us tomorrow.…[W]e will make those Union Men cry for quarter yet.…I am in hurry will finish after the battle is won and let you know we have whipped them."[237]

Lyon sent orders after midnight to his Volunteer Regiment and Home Guard commanders to assemble at the arsenal in the morning.[238] A heavy morning rain interfered, however, as likely did the logistics of getting so many men out of their homes. Blair didn't arrive with his men until late

The bronze relief on the back of the base of the Lyon statue in Lyon Park depicts the surrender of Camp Jackson. The neighboring Anheuser-Busch Brewery was founded by two of the volunteers in Lyon's troops that day. *Peter Downs.*

Saint Louis University stopped calling the campus east of Grand Avenue "Frost Campus" in the early 2010s. The name had honored the general who lost to Union forces at Camp Jackson. *Peter Downs.*

morning, and it wasn't until 1:00 p.m. that Lyon began marching his men—estimates vary from seven thousand to eight thousand—away from the arsenal grounds.[239]

While Lyon waited for his men to assemble, Colonel John Bowen of the Missouri Volunteer Militia arrived with a letter from Frost asking Lyon if he planned to attack Camp Jackson and arguing the legality of the militia gathering. Lyon refused to accept it.[240]

Lyon had Camp Jackson completely surrounded by 3:00 p.m. and demanded Frost's immediate surrender. Frost decided to play the victim. "I never for a moment having conceived the idea that so illegal and unconstitutional a demand as I have received from you would be made by an officer of the United States Army, I am wholly unprepared to defend my command from this unwarranted attack, and shall therefore be forced to comply with your demand," he wrote.[241]

Today that area is part of St. Louis University. From 1960 until the mid-2010s, it was named Frost Campus in honor of the state militia commander and future Confederate general.

Some historians have claimed Lyon's attack was not necessary,[242] but Grant credited Lyon and Blair for quick thinking in saving a major arsenal from Confederate hands. "If St. Louis had been captured by the rebels, it would have made a vast difference in our war….Instead of a campaign before Vicksburg, it would have been a campaign before St. Louis," he later wrote.[243]

18

OLIVE STREET

Olive Street was a magnet for marching men in the early days of the Civil War in St. Louis. It was the route an estimated eight hundred state militia volunteers took to march to Camp Jackson after gathering at Olive and Sixth Streets on May 6. Drums rolled. Crowds of friends and family members lined the route and cheered them on, generating feelings of excitement and romance.

One state militiaman, John McNamara, later recalled the exhilaration of the march, writing in his memoir: "Tramp, tramp! through crowds of admiring citizens. Tramping, tramping! to 'The Girl I Left Behind Me'… Tramp! tramp! into Lindell's Grove. Tramp! tramp! to the air of Dixie…."[244]

Four days later, they were marched back down Olive Street as prisoners, escorted by Blair's regiment, the First U.S. Volunteers.[245] A large crowd gathered to see what was happening. Many people were just curious; others came to support the secessionists. Many men walked around St. Louis armed in those days. Some of the men in the crowd waved pistols in the air, some cheered Jefferson Davis and hurled rocks and insults at the German volunteers.[246]

Numerous incidents erupted up and down the street.[247] A crowd surged around an artillery battery separating it from the column of soldiers. A regular army officer ordered his men to fix bayonets and clear a path to the battery. Some of the men fired into the air and were ordered to stop. Farther down the line, someone stepped out of the crowd and fired three shots at a U.S. Army captain. A soldier lunged forward and bayoneted him

The Lyon statue in Lyon Park originally was installed on Olive Street at the site of Camp Jackson, but St. Louis University had it removed in 1960 when the university purchased the area and renamed it Frost Campus, after the general who lost to Lyon. *Peter Downs.*

as he took aim to fire a fourth shot. Some of the untrained Union militiamen fired into the crowd when threatened. A drunk turned back from the line of militiamen, pulled a gun and started firing, prompting a return volley over the heads of the gathered crowd.

Someone in a crowd near Camp Jackson shot at soldiers guarding prisoners, and more joined in when the soldiers returned fire. Another crowd gathered around a man who pulled a pistol and urged a coordinated attack on the soldiers. The initial attack saw an army doctor and a captain fall, and soldiers began taking fire from both sides of the street. There were at least two reports of prisoners pulling out concealed handguns in the confusion and joining the fight, as well as several reports of frightened, untrained Union militiamen firing indiscriminately into the crowds from which shots erupted. Many in the crowds were caught in crossfires.

By the time Lyon and his officers got their men back under control, twenty-seven people lay dead or dying where the crowds had been, three of the prisoners had been killed and four Union officers and troops were dead or dying and another ten wounded. For the untrained Germans, the insults, projectiles and finally gunfire must have brought to mind and heart memories of the abuse they had taken for years from their self-styled betters in St. Louis, stories of battles lost in the German states in 1848 and the battle over Soulard ballot boxes.

The "St. Louis Massacre" became a rallying cry for secessionists in Missouri and proved that "conditional Unionism" was an unstable position. It made many men who had tried to straddle the divide between North and South finally take sides.

Celebrated St. Louis lawyer Uriel Wright—he once represented a woman who sued Henry Shaw for $100,000 for breaking an implied promise to marry[248]—was elected to the state convention on secession as an Unconditional Unionist. After the Camp Jackson events, however, he was so upset by the killing of white citizens by Germans that he left St. Louis and threw in with the South. He served as a major in the Confederate army.[249] His friend and neighbor, a slave owner and Conditional Unionist name Thomas Skinker (after whom Skinker Avenue it named) stayed in St. Louis.[250] John Knapp, commander of Frost's First Regiment at Camp Jackson, joined the Unionist Missouri State Guard under Governor Gamble and in 1864 led a brigade in pursuit of Confederate general Sterling Price.[251]

But where some saw tragedy, others saw opportunity. George P. Dorriss, for example, had a thriving trade in enslaved people based in Platte County in western Missouri. He had a dungeon on his farm where he kept enslaved people until he had enough for a caravan south. The two years before the Civil War were the golden years for his trade in enslaved people.[252] After war broke out, however, he gave up the slave trade and moved to St. Louis to sell supplies to the U.S. Army. The army contracts and loan-sharking made him a millionaire by the war's end.[253]

As much as some white St. Louisans were appalled by what happened at Camp Jackson, some African Americans were thrilled.[254] Two enslaved girls, for example, reportedly taunted a Southern sympathizer on the street with gleeful cries of "They've got all your tents."[255]

Five weeks later, there was another battle on Olive, this one at Olive and Seventh Streets, when snipers opened fire on five companies of Home Guards, now formally part of the U.S. Army as the U.S. Army Reserve Corps. Two soldiers were wounded, including a company commander.

Galusha Anderson described the Home Guards as "raw and undisciplined," and, being German, "They had become sensitive and vindictive under the stinging taunts which had been wantonly hurled at them by their hostile neighbors." When fired on, "evidently without a moment's thought," some of them returned fire at what they thought was the source, the second story of a building on Seventh Street, killing five.[256]

The building they fired at was the Recorder's Court. Some historians think the sniper or snipers were in the building next door.[257]

WALNUT AND FIFTH STREETS

Some secessionists, according to Anderson, were determined to avenge the loss of Camp Jackson. The opportunity came when news spread that a regiment of north-side Germans was getting enrolled at the St. Louis Arsenal and would have to march through downtown to return to their regimental base and homes on the north side.[258]

The regiment was Colonel Charles Stifel's Fifth Regiment of the U.S. Reserve Corps. They had not participated in the capture of Camp Jackson, as they had not been enrolled into reserve corps. They were mustered in and given arms on May 11.[259] The men were mostly laborers with little weapons experience. Although Stifel had begun drilling men at night in the malthouse of his brewery at Howard and North Fourteenth Streets months before, he had only twenty-five muskets for over one thousand men.[260]

Secessionists gathered at the Presbyterian church at Fifth and Walnut Streets and in and around the houses on the other side of Walnut Street. When the green troops of the Fifth turned on to Walnut Street, the mob began throwing stones at them and threatening them with knives. As the line of marching soldiers stretched from Seventh to Fifth Streets, shots rang out and several soldiers fell. Many of these men may never have had muskets in their hands before, but now they used them. They blindly returned fire. Six civilians were killed. Two of the reservists also died.[261]

Above: Stifel's volunteers were ambushed by attackers shielded by the columns of the Presbyterian church at Fifth and Walnut. This is an 1868 photo by Thomas M. Easterly. *Missouri Historical Society.*

Opposite: *Harper's Weekly* illustration of the attack on Stifel's volunteers. *Missouri Historical Society.*

UNITED STATES VOLUNTEERS ATTACKED BY THE MOB, CORNER OF FIFTH AND WALNUT STREETS, ST. LOUIS, MISSOURI.—[SKETCHED BY M. HASTINGS, ESQ.]

In the aftermath, Galusha Anderson wrote, "Feeling on both sides ran high. It was intense, bitter, hot....Apprehension of something awful pervaded many minds."[262]

20

THE PLANTER'S HOUSE HOTEL

G eneral Harney thought he could reduce the tension. He returned to St. Louis on May 11, still in command, still aiming for a peaceful settlement in Missouri and still tuned to the fears of the city's social and economic elite.

A coalition of the elite that included "anti-Republican" Mayor Daniel Taylor and leading Conditional Unionists like Hamilton Gamble demanded of Harney that he suppress the German Home Guards. The old French and Southern families both feared and loathed the Germans, whom they always referred to as "Dutch" with all the derision their voices could muster. Well-bred ladies in polite society were known to refer to them as "Amsterdam Dutch without the Amster."[263]

Harney promised to disarm the German American Home Guards or transfer them out of the city,[264] but Blair reminded him that Lincoln had personally ordered the formation of reserve corps and had instructed Lyon to do so in cooperation with the Committee of Safety. The committee wanted them armed and in the city.[265]

Unable to move the Home Guards out of the city, Harney ordered regular troops from Jefferson Barracks into the city and deployed them with artillery in the German American wards to contain the Germans.[266] This might have pleased Gamble and his brother-in-law, Attorney General Bates, as Bates had supported the anti-immigrant American Party, but it could not have pleased Blair or Lincoln, both of whom had cultivated German American voters for support. Lincoln quietly sent Blair an order removing Harney from command and giving him leeway as to when to use it.[267]

The Planter's House Hotel as seen from Fourth Street in front of the federal courthouse in 1867. Stereogram by Boehl & Koenig. *Missouri Historical Society.*

Meanwhile, Harney continued to act as if secession was less of a threat than German revolution. He had called a military bill passed by the state legislature illegal and an "indirect secession ordinance"[268] but did nothing to interfere with it. Instead, he made an agreement with General Sterling Price, the new commanding general of the state militia, to keep the U.S. Army in St. Louis and let Price "maintain order" everywhere else in the state.[269] Price used the time to send out recruiters for the Missouri Volunteer Militia and organize new regiments.

Harney and Blair both got reports about secessionist activities across the state and hostile acts against Unionists and against federal authority. Blair sent them to his brother in Washington and to the War Department. Harney sent them to Price and accepted Price's assurances that he was attending to those matters.[270]

Even Lincoln became exasperated with Harney's inaction.[271] Then Blair decided on May 30 that the time had come to use the president's order. He relieved Harney of command and made Lyon his temporary replacement. That change in command set the stage for an eventful meeting on June 11 at the Planter's House Hotel on Fourth Street between Lyon and Blair on one side and Price and Governor Jackson on the other.

The Planter's House, a three-hundred-room, four-story luxury hotel, was the pride of the St. Louis elite, who boasted that it was the finest hotel in the West. It took up the entire block north of the courthouse on the west side of Fourth Street between Chestnut and Pine Streets. Its name was synonymous with luxury and good service. It housed expensive shops and four restaurants, and the detailed decorations in the grand ballroom were modeled on a Greek temple.[272] Frank and Montgomery Blair had lived there for a time with their wives. Brown had lived there. Lincoln stayed there when visiting St. Louis, as did William Sherman.

It was Governor Jackson who insisted on meeting in the hotel. Lyon wanted to meet at the arsenal. He wanted the governor to commit to the Union. The governor wanted Lyon to cease enlisting troops, disband the Home Guard and pledge not to deploy Federal troops anywhere in the state where they were not already stationed. After four hours of fruitless talks, Lyon angrily left the meeting. One of the governor's aides wrote decades later that Lyon stalked out saying the governor's demands "meant war."[273]

PART III

MANAGING ST. LOUIS DURING THE WAR

21

CAMP ETHIOPIA

General Samuel Curtis, then Union commander in Missouri, established a refugee camp for fugitive enslaved people on Laclede's Landing nicknamed "Camp Ethiopia." Slaveholders claimed that the very existence of the camp encouraged enslaved people to escape their captivity.[274]

Curtis was spurred into action by the arrival of a steamboat from Helena, Arkansas, in March 1863. On board were U.S. Army chaplain Samuel Sawyer and five hundred formerly enslaved people seeking refuge. City officials and slavery advocates demanded he turn them away. They suggested that the contrabands, as they were called, would not be safe if he let them stay.[275]

Curtis first protested their arrival but then quickly decided to make a very public show of support for the refugees. He paraded them under the protection of Union soldiers to the prominent location he had picked to house them: the site of Missouri's first legislative assembly, the Missouri Hotel at Morgan and Main (now First) Streets.[276] The number of refugees housed in the hotel soon swelled to 1,500.

Mary Meachum and the group that would take the name the Colored Ladies Contraband Relief Society may have taken the lead in providing assistance to the refugees. They would have been among the first to learn about the arrival of the refugee boat, due to the strength of the African Baptist churches among riverboat and levee workers. They would have sprung into action immediately while the white Ladies Union Aid Society was bogged down in arguments over what to do. The leaders of that society

Drawing of the Missouri Hotel, circa 1830. The hotel became a refugee camp in the Civil War. *Missouri Historical Society*.

The Missouri Hotel was demolished shortly after the Civil War and replaced by this six-story building. *Peter Downs*.

opposed aiding refugees, leading to the split in the organization and the subsequent formation of a (white) Ladies Contraband Relief Society.[277]

Meachum and her white allies turned a nearby building into a hospital, opened a school in a neighboring church and opened a kitchen to prepare food.[278] The Ladies Union Aid Society lost so many members over the issue that the leadership reversed course after a year and embraced the cause of contraband relief.

Sawyer and the contraband relief societies found work for the adult men on the levees—undoubtedly aided by Meachum's ties to a network of levee workers—and on fortifications around the city and shortly found private employment for three hundred of them. Work brought pay, which allowed people to buy their own food and, in the case of those with private jobs, move off the levee and free space for new arrivals.[279]

The same parts of society that wanted General Harney to move German American volunteers out of the city now wanted the refugee camp removed from the city center. Barely two months after Curtis had established Camp Ethiopia, Governor Gamble's complaints to Washington had an effect. Lincoln replaced Curtis with Schofield, who moved the highly visible refugee camp to an out-of-the-way spot outside the city by Benton Barracks. That also moved the refugees away from jobs and made it more difficult for Meachum and others to provide them with assistance.

ST. VINCENT DE PAUL CATHOLIC CHURCH AND ST. JOHN THE APOSTLE AND EVANGELIST

Father Hennessey of St. Vincent de Paul Catholic Church, near Tenth Street and Park Avenue, met with provost marshals in 1862 at the urging of his archbishop, Peter Richard Kenrick.[280] Martial law had made the provost marshals responsible for investigating many ordinarily civilian disagreements, but the disputes often were cast in terms of someone aiding the enemy.

The provost marshals had contacted the archbishop for an explanation for newspaper reports that Hennessey had preached, "Unionists would all go to hell and the secessionists to heaven." Kenrick made sure Hennessey talked to the military police, perhaps with a little coaching first. He was probably irked by the affair. He couldn't afford for it to be true.

Archbishop Kenrick was desperately trying to keep the church neutral and balance the conflicting loyalties of the French and Virginian aristocratic, Southern-leaning families who funded many church projects and the more numerous German and laboring population of parishioners. He didn't even preach for the first two years of the war for fear people would twist his words to support one side or the other. His only public statements were calls for civility and prayer.[281]

People still had their suspicions, however. It didn't help that the parishioners of both the old cathedral and the new one, St. John the Apostle and Evangelist Church, were mainly wealthy secessionists. Neither did it help that Kenrick had refused Father Peter De Smet's request to be allowed to serve as a Union chaplain,[282] while Father John Bannon, the pastor of

St. Vincent de Paul Catholic Church looks much the same now as it did during the Civil War. *Peter Downs*.

A parishioner at St. Vincent's thought the priest said, "Unionists would all go to hell and secessionists to heaven." Photo by Emil Boehl. *Missouri Historical Society*.

St. John the Apostle and another Irishman, had gotten captured at Camp Jackson and later ran away to join the Confederate army.

St. John the Apostle and Evangelist Church was on the northeast corner of Sixteenth and Chestnut Streets. It served the tony Lucas Place development (now Locust Street), St. Louis's first exclusive neighborhood.[283] Influential residents of the Place included a U.S. senator (Trusten Polk, a proslavery Democrat who resigned his seat on January 10, 1862, and joined the Confederate army), a former mayor (John How) and General William Harney. Father Bannon was the pastor of the church.[284] He officiated at the wedding of Daniel Taylor, the anti-Republican mayor of St. Louis in 1861 with ties to the Chouteau family.[285]

Bannon was chaplain to Company E, the Washington Blues, in the Missouri Volunteer Militia and unofficial chaplain to Company D, Emmet and Montgomery Guards.[286] He had visited the guard at Camp Jackson and was captured by Unionist forces under Captain Lyon.[287] It wasn't an accident. Bannon visited the wealthy Lucas family, the developers of Lucas Place, on December 15, 1861, put on a disguise and slipped out the back door with two companions to join Price's army in southwest Missouri.[288]

Bannon did not agree with Kenrick's desire to keep the Catholic Church neutral. He preached against the North and abolitionism. He described the fight between the North and South as a holy war, a battle between "the cross and the crescent," with the South cast in the role of the last bastion of Christian civilization and Northerners as "infidels."

Bannon was with Bowen's First Missouri Confederate Brigade when he was captured again at Vicksburg. Grant released him, and he traveled to Richmond to meet with Confederate president Jefferson Davis, who sent him on a mission to Ireland to discourage Irish immigration to the United States without revealing that he was paid by the Confederate States.[289] He went to Rome in 1864 to urge the pope to support the South.[290]

Having one priest run off to join the Confederate army raised some doubts about Kenrick's neutrality but could be dismissed as an aberration. A second such priest might seem like a pattern. So Kenrick arranged for Hennessey to meet with the provost marshals. He probably had him coached first and may even have helped line up statements to support his story. They knew what the allegations were; they had been in the press after all.

The allegations against Hennessey stemmed from complaints Catherine Bockman made to her neighbors. She went to Mass at St. Vincent's on May 27, 1862, to pray for her husband, a Union soldier in the Fifth Missouri Cavalry, and she heard Hennessey preach that Unionists would

Right: The pastor of St. John the Apostle and Evangelist ran away to join the Confederate army and later acted as the Confederacy's emissary to the Vatican. *Missouri Historical Society*.

Below: St. John the Apostle and Evangelist Catholic Church is still in use. *Peter Downs*.

all go to hell. The southside German community was outraged and loudly denounced the priest.[291]

It was all a misunderstanding, Hennessey assured the provost marshals. She just didn't understand his words, because, well, you know, these immigrants don't always understand English. He didn't preach about secession, he preached about the ascension. And it wasn't Unionists he said were going to hell; it was Unitarians who were going to hell.[292]

The provost marshals were satisfied. The charges were dismissed, the case was closed and a sigh of relief came from Archbishop Kenrick.

GRATIOT STREET PRISON / McDOWELL MEDICAL COLLEGE

The U.S. Army turned the McDowell Medical College at Eighth and Gratiot Streets into the Gratiot Street Prison in December 1861.[293] The site of the prison is now part of a rail line on the north edge of the Purina campus.

Federal troops seized McDowell Medical College in 1861 after Dr. Joseph Nash McDowell ran off to join the Confederacy. The government used it as a barracks before converting it into a military prison.

It was a stout building, probably because McDowell had a fortress in mind when he built it in 1848. It consisted of two brick wings connected by a three-story, octagonal brick tower. McDowell had it constructed with gun placements and reinforced walls to repel a possible mass assault. He bought four cannons to mount in the placements and purchased numerous muskets, rumored to be as many as 1,500.[294]

McDowell was loudly anti-Catholic and anti-immigrant, but he especially hated Germans and anyone opposed to slavery. He threatened to blow up any German American who tried to enter the college,[295] talked of launching an attack on Mexico and claimed that abolitionists taught "black men to murder white men…and violate white women."[296] The formation of the Confederate States of America in February 1861 gave McDowell a focus for his fanaticism. He gave belligerently pro-Confederate speeches from the street corner by his college, berated pro-Union colleagues and secretly shipped his weapons collection south.[297]

McDowell Medical College, which the U.S. Army turned into a prison in 1861, was later torn down for the route of a railway bridge across the Mississippi. *Missouri Historical Society.*

The Unionist victory at Camp Jackson was a sign to McDowell that it was time to leave St. Louis. He and his son Drake took his two cannons and headed for Arkansas to join the Confederate army.[298] His head surgeon, Dr. William McPheeters, joined the Confederate army a year later.[299]

The Gratiot Street Military Prison held Confederate prisoners of war, spies, guerillas, civilians suspected of disloyalty and even Union soldiers accused of criminal conduct. It housed both men and women.[300] Security in the early days was so lax that one prisoner escaped by simply walking past the guards while carrying a toolbox and wearing clothing borrowed from a carpenter. Another blackened his face and hands with chimney soot and walked out carrying an empty coal bucket.[301] Although security increased, inmates continued to try to escape.

Sixty prisoners escaped through a tunnel on December 19, 1863. They had discovered a concealed cellar in the prison, cut through the brick wall and tunneled forty feet underneath the prison yard and sergeant's yard and house to the cellar of a neighboring two-story house. They exited the house on Gratiot Street and walked away. More would have escaped, but one prisoner made a wrong turn after getting out and headed toward the Schofield Barracks. He stumbled into guards, who then discovered the tunnel.[302]

Conditions at the prison varied with crowding and the season. The number of inmates seesawed from fewer than five hundred to more than one thousand.[303] Some prisoners said they were treated well; others complained about the coffee and that they got only two meals a day. There were no reports of physical abuse, but complaints were registered about the way the guards talked about Southern women. The quality of cleanliness, maintenance and ventilation varied with crowding.[304]

EADS'S UNION MARINE WORKS

J ames Eads's Union Marine Works in Carondelet has as good a claim as any place to be the pivot point that determined the outcome of the Civil War.

War west of the Appalachian Mountains was less theatrical than it was in the mid-Atlantic states. Battles in the mid-Atlantic states were conducted under the gazes of politicians, foreign governments, the press and, thus, the broad public. They were as much about public relations and diplomacy as about military advantage. Battles in the West were primarily about military advantage. As long as the armies of the United States and the Confederate States could protect their nation's capitals, the real strategic battles were fought in the Mississippi River basin.[305] The key to controlling the basin was the Mississippi River itself. The Union Marine Works gave the Union the key to controlling the river.

General-in-Chief Winfield Scott wanted to make control of the Mississippi the major objective of the war. With it, the Union could blockade the South and, like a giant snake wrapped around its throat, eventually strangle it. He called his plan the Anaconda Plan.[306] Attorney General Bates, the first cabinet minister from west of the Mississippi, also urged a war strategy centered on the Mississippi River valley,[307] as did the governors of Illinois, Indiana, Michigan, Ohio, New York and Pennsylvania.[308] As the U.S. Navy imposed a blockade on the South's Atlantic and Confederate ports, two-way traffic developed across the Mississippi through Texas to Matamoros, Mexico. Cotton exports moved west, and gold, silver and war materiel moved east.[309]

An interpretive marker at St. Louis Square Park on South Broadway at West Courtois Street commemorates the construction of ironclads in Carondelet. *Peter Downs.*

Ironclads sailing past Cairo, Illinois, in 1863. *Naval History and Heritage Command.*

The Union needed to control the southern Mississippi River to effectively blockade the South. Bates and governors of what were then the northwestern U.S. states also were convinced that whoever controlled the lower reaches of the river would eventually control the upper reaches as well, because so much of the produce and production of the northwestern states still moved down the river. They could not permit the Southern Mississippi River states to secede for fear of losing their own independence and becoming an economic tail of the Southern dog.[310] If a Southern victory threatened the Northwest, it would also threaten the Union's hold on California.

In short, much hinged on control of the Mississippi River. The Confederacy built fortifications on the riverbanks to control use of the river.[311] The Union countered them with ironclad gunboats. James Eads built those gunboats. The Union won. The gunboats were able to enforce a blockade and also opened up rivers as highways for the massive, rapid movement of armies into the heart of the Confederacy.

James Eads's Union Marine Works was between Marceau Street and the north bank of River Des Peres at the confluence with the Mississippi River. Tracks, cranes and a railway engine were used to move the boats in and out of the river. The tracks extended from a shed where eight hundred shipwrights and laborers assembled the boats, down a shallow slope and into the river, where the boats were launched.

The USS *Carondelet*, built in Carondelet, was the first ironclad constructed for the United States. It was launched three months before the more famous USS *Monitor*. The USS *St. Louis*, USS *Louisville* and USS *Pittsburgh* soon followed.[312]

Eads's company had never before built a boat when he contracted to construct them in six weeks for a cost of $89,600 each.[313] The bidding for the contract was overseen by one of Frank Blair's brothers-in-law, Quartermaster General Montgomery Meigs.[314] Eads's bid was the lowest, but in the end the cost was $101,808 each.[315]

Eads got involved in the project three days after the start of the war, in May 1861, when Attorney General Bates asked him to come to Washington to explain the importance of closing the Ohio River to the Confederacy at Cairo, Illinois, to prevent the South from using the Ohio to launch attacks deep into the Union.[316] Eads was a self-taught civil engineer who had made a fortune designing steam-powered salvage vessels equipped with his patented diving bell.[317] His home on the west side of Compton Avenue, between Susan and Henrietta Streets,[318] was not far from Bates's Grape Hill estate.

The rails to carry newly built gunboats to the river at the Union Marine Works were still visible in 1885. Photo by D.C. Humphreys. *Missouri Historical Society.*

Eads made two visits to Washington. He met once with Secretary of the Navy Gideon Welles and another time with Lincoln and the cabinet to explain his ideas for using armed boats on rivers. He also submitted his ideas in writing to the navy. One of his ideas was to convert salvage vessels into "floating batteries."[319]

Secretary of War Simon Cameron sent Eads to Cincinnati to meet with General George B. McClellan, then commanding the Department of the Ohio. Cameron sent along a message that he thought Eads's proposal was a good one, but the decision was McClellan's to make.[320] Welles sent Commander John Rodgers to consult with McClellan as well. Eads and Rodgers convinced McClellan that at least three boats would be needed to seal the Ohio at Cairo. Eads suggested converting three of his boats. McClellan detailed Rodgers to inspect Eads's boats and either buy them or make arrangements to buy others. Rodgers, an ocean sailor, was unimpressed with Eads's boats and eventually settled on three in Cincinnati.[321]

Meanwhile, the Naval Bureau of Construction and Repair sketched out some specifications for purpose-built river warcraft. Naval engineer Samuel Pook was assigned to modify them so the government could advertise for bids for construction. Frank Blair knew about the plan and urged Meigs to reach out to Eads.[322] Meigs approved the specifications in July. Many boatbuilders competed for the job, but Eads's bid was the lowest and promised the fastest delivery.[323]

The former site of the Union Marine Works is being prepared for the construction of an industrial park. *Peter Downs*.

These boats acquired the nickname "Pook's Turtles." Each boat was flat-bottomed, 175 feet long and 50 feet wide. The sloping walls of the deckhouse or casemate were made of two and a half inches of iron plate on top of twenty-six inches of oak. Each boat carried thirteen guns: three firing forward, four on each side and two in the rear. Each boat was crewed by 160 officers and men.[324]

The bidding for Pook's Turtles occurred about the time that General John Frémont arrived in St. Louis. Frémont, who met with both Lincoln and General Scott before heading to St. Louis, was convinced that he was supposed to focus his energies on preparing for a campaign down the Mississippi River.[325] That may be why he thought securing Cairo was more important than securing Springfield. In any event, he and Eads soon hit it off.

Frémont decided, without the approval of the War Department, to buy the salvage vessels from Eads that Rodgers had deemed unworthy and contracted with Eads to convert them to armored gunboats.[326] The largest was the 633-ton *Benton*. Once converted from a snag boat, the armored paddle wheeler carried sixteen guns.[327] Rodgers's successor praised it as worth three of Pook's Turtles.[328] It was prized for its greater power and maneuverability on the lower Mississippi River than that of the Turtles.[329]

Eads discovered, however, that a promise to pay was not the same thing as payment. The War Department did not make its scheduled payments. Meigs confessed to Bates that his department wasn't prepared for wartime contracting. The money Congress appropriated for river gunboats got diverted to more pressing needs. Eads, an ardent Unionist, used up his business credit and took on large personal loans to keep construction moving. The War Department didn't start making its payments until after Congress appropriated more money for gunboats in December 1861.[330]

Eads delivered the Turtles in January 1862. They took part in the Union campaign that captured Forts Henry and Donelson in Tennessee; New Madrid, Missouri; and Island Number 10 in the spring of 1862. At the time of the battles, the boats were technically still owned by Eads. The government didn't finish paying for them until June.[331]

They helped take Fort Pillow on June 4, 1862, and destroyed the Confederate's river fleet at Memphis on June 6. They were instrumental in the siege of Vicksburg, which surrendered in July 1863. Two of the ironclads led Admiral David Farragut's capture of Mobile Bay.[332]

The War Department was so taken with the success of Eads's river gunboats by mid-1862 that it contracted for a class of lighter ironclads for

General Frémont contracted with James Eads for a bigger ironclad, the USS *Benton*. Photo by George Holmes Bixby, 1864. *Naval History and Heritage Command.*

Some skilled workers at the Union Marine Works lived in stone cottages such as this one on East Steins Street. *Peter Downs.*

the Tennessee and Cumberland Rivers. Eads built six boats in the class. They drew only three and half feet of water when fully loaded. The gunwales rose only six inches above the waterline. Eads replaced the gunports of Pook's Turtles with a revolving gun turret that contained two eleven-inch guns. Eads had his own turret design, but the War Department was impressed with the design used on the *Monitor*. They compromised, and Eads installed one of each design on the two-turret boats.[333]

Eads kept adding to the Union Marine Works as he won contracts for more ironclads. At its peak, the Carondelet site included a gas plant and seventy forges. The boatyard and machine shops buzzed with the activity of nine hundred workers. With Eads paying out $15,000 a week in wages,[334] the workers earned an average of $16.67 a week.

Blacksmiths produced red-hot rivets at the forges. They tossed the rivets to boys as soon as they made them. They boys caught them in cans and ran them to shipwrights to hammer home.[335] If a boy missed a catch, he was liable to get a serious burn on his arm, leg or body.

Some of the workers may have lived in the small stone houses that dotted the lowlands near the river in Carondelet. These houses were built in the 1840s and 1850s, sometimes by the stonemasons who first lived in them.[336]

The workers at the ironworks joined a citywide strike in April 1864 protesting the loss of purchasing power due to inflation and employers replacing men with lower-paid women and boys. General William Rosecrans, commander of the Union forces in Missouri, broke the strike when he declared it illegal and a disruption of the war effort. He banned labor unions and ordered employers to give his command the names of strikers so soldiers could arrest them.[337]

There is an Eads interpretative sign at St. Louis Square Park on South Broadway at Courtois Street.

25

JEFFERSON BARRACKS
HISTORIC SITE

Jefferson Barracks was the cradle of Civil War generals. More than two hundred of the war's generals served at Jefferson Barracks during part of their pre–Civil War army career.[338] Among them were the following: Robert E. Lee, James Longstreet, Albert Sidney Johnston, Joseph E. Johnston, Braxton Bragg, George Edward Pickett, Edmund Kirby Smith, J.E.B. Stuart, Jefferson Davis, Ulysses S Grant, William T. Sherman, Henry Halleck, Philip Sheridan, Don Carlos Buell, Grenville Dodge, Winfield Scott Hancock, Montgomery Meigs and George McClellan.[339]

Among the actions that Captain Lyon took to defend the cache of Union arms in St. Louis was to detail troops from his force at the arsenal to defend the powder magazine at the barracks in April 1861.[340] That building now houses the Old Ordnance Room Museum. The stables were built in 1851 to house horses and wagons used to carry munitions from the arsenal in St. Louis to the magazines. The laborer's house, just north of the stables, also built in 1851, was used by civilian workers employed at the ordnance depot.

Jefferson Barracks continued to serve as a training site for new soldiers in 1861, but that training was shifted to Benton Barracks north of St. Louis once it opened.

The main mission of Jefferson Barracks during the Civil War was as a military hospital. The army, with the help of the Western Sanitary Commission, initially rented a five-story building across from the federal courthouse on the southwest corner of Fifth (now Broadway) and Chestnut

Congress passed legislation to convert the cemetery at Jefferson Barracks to a national cemetery on July 17, 1862. *Peter Downs.*

(the site is currently part of Kiener Plaza) for a 1,500-bed hospital in autumn 1861 as wounded from battles in southwest Missouri filled the existing hospitals in the city.[341] That proved insufficient, and the barracks were turned over to the army's medical department in March 1862.[342] A general hospital opened a month later, just in time to receive wounded from the Battle of Shiloh, from which 7,882 were sent by boat up the Mississippi River to St. Louis.[343]

The Western Sanitary Commission raised $770,000 to fund the expansion of hospital facilities at the post.[344] Three months later, the expansion to 2,500 beds was complete. Another 2,500-bed hospital was built at Benton Barracks when the first two hospitals proved insufficient for the number of sick and wounded soldiers, both Union and Confederate, being sent to St. Louis.

General Frémont, acting on the advice of his wife, Jessie, authorized the creation of the Western Sanitary Commission to assist and advise army medical teams west of the Mississippi River on September 5, 1861.[345] The original five members included William Greenleaf Eliot, a prominent Unitarian minister and founder of Washington University and of Mary Institute.[346] Their innovations included the outfitting of the first railroad hospital cars in the United States in October 1861 and the conversion of a

Nathaniel Lyon detailed Frank Blair to remove the gunpowder stored in this building at Jefferson Barracks and bring it to the arsenal in St. Louis. *Peter Downs*.

The stable and laborer's house at Jefferson Barracks, built in the 1851. *Peter Downs*.

The northeast part of Kiener Plaza is where the U.S. War Department had a five-story hospital during the Civil War and the Western Sanitary Commission had its offices. *Peter Downs.*

steamboat into a floating hospital or hospital ship in 1862, both designed to provide intensive medical care closer to soldiers at the front.[347]

The Western Sanitary Commission held a large fair on Twelfth Street (now Tucker Boulevard) between Olive and St. Charles to raise additional funds for medical care and refugee relief in May and June 1864.[348] Net proceeds came to $554,000. The bulk of the money went to hospitals and group homes for wounded soldiers, but $1,000 a month was allocated to the St. Louis Colored Ladies Contraband Relief Society for its work with African American refugees.[349]

The fair was notable as an experiment in integration that did not survive post-Reconstruction. African Americans came and went through the same entrances as whites and were served at the same booths and counters. African American soldiers provided security.

To Anderson, who was actively involved in the work of the Western Sanitary Commission, "It looked like a revolution when we saw, in a slave State, white women of high social standing, without complaint or murmur, sell articles to colored purchasers."[350] Not everyone was as pleased as he was.

The wounded and sick typically came to St. Louis from battlefields by steamboat. At times, there were more sick and wounded soldiers at the

Above: Over ten thousand Civil War dead from battlefields across Missouri and Arkansas are buried at Jefferson Barracks cemetery. Many of the remains were not identified. *Peter Downs*.

Left: A total of 175 African American soldiers died of cholera when they returned to St. Louis to be mustered out after the war. *Peter Downs*.

Jefferson Barracks hospital than at any other hospital in the nation. Those who died were buried in the post cemetery.

Congress passed legislation to convert the post cemetery to a national cemetery on July 17, 1862. Union and Confederate soldiers who died in the hospital were buried there, as were soldiers who died of smallpox and other contagious diseases on Quarantine Island, an island that used to sit in the Mississippi River four miles south of downtown St. Louis. General Sherman ordered Union dead in battlefields in Missouri and Arkansas to be reinterred at Jefferson Barracks National Cemetery in 1865.[351]

The cemetery includes a monument to the Fifty-Sixth Infantry Regiment, United States Colored Troops. The Fifty-Sixth was originally organized in St. Louis as the Third Arkansas Infantry Regiment (African Descent).[352] It was named an Arkansas regiment instead of a Missouri regiment because Governor Gamble feared the reaction of slaveholders in the state to the arming of African Americans.[353] The regiment served mostly in Arkansas. Of the regiment's casualties (2 officers and 647 enlisted men), 96 percent resulted from cholera contracted on the trip back to St. Louis from Arkansas to be mustered out in 1866.[354]

In addition to Union dead, more than one thousand Confederate dead are buried at the cemetery. A Confederate monument was erected in their honor in 1988.

BENTON BARRACKS

G eneral Frémont ordered the construction of Benton Barracks in August 1861 after new recruits from Illinois, Indiana, Iowa and Ohio began arriving in St. Louis for training.[355] A hospital was added later.

The barracks consisted of continuous rows of low frame buildings forming a big rectangle. Each company had its own quarters separated from its neighbors by framed partitions. Each company's quarters contained two rows of bunks. Behind and detached from each company's quarters was another framed structure designed to serve as the company kitchen with a brick oven for cooking with openings for kettles, pots, boilers, etc.[356] Leander Stillwell, a corporal from Carrollton, Illinois, in the Sixty-First Illinois Volunteer Infantry, described the barracks as "greatly superior to our home-made shacks at Carrollton."[357]

F.F. Kiner, a first sergeant in the Fourteenth Iowa Volunteer Infantry, praised the design and construction of the barracks. He was particularly impressed with the pipes for running water in every company kitchen and the site drainage that prevented the grounds from staying muddy for long after rains. "I never saw any better in all my travels as a soldier, and doubt much if there is any better of the kind in the United States," he wrote.[358]

A 2,500-bed hospital, one of the largest military hospitals in the country, was added to Benton Barracks in 1863.

Benton Barracks became a major training ground for African American soldiers after Order No. 135 of November 1863 allowed the enlistment

CAMP BENTON (St. Louis)

Camp Benton, or "Benton Barracks," as it was generally known, was established in 1861 on the Fair Grounds in St. Louis by General John Charles Frémont, and served as a training camp and military hospital throughout the Civil War. The grounds, now Fairgrounds Park, were the site of the Agricultural and Mechanical Association fairs from 1855 to 1860, and from 1865 to 1904. The above picture is taken from a letter dated October 24, 1863; it is from a lithograph by Alexander McLean, whose firm is listed in St. Louis directories from 1851 to 1866.

General Frémont established Camp Benton to train new recruits for the Civil War. Lithograph by Alexander McLean (1863). *Missouri Historical Society.*

of enslaved men without the consent of their masters.[359] The Black units formally organized for service at Benton Barracks were the First, Second, Third and Fourth Missouri Colored Infantry[360] and companies G, H, I and K of the First Iowa Colored Infantry. Only 440 of the 1,000 men in the First Iowa came from Iowa, and many of them had escaped slavery in Missouri.[361]

Other states also sought to enlist African American men in Missouri. The majority of the 2,080 soldiers of the Kansas Colored Troops were from Missouri. There were only 126 African American men of military age (eighteen to forty-five) in Kansas in 1860, according to the U.S. census. Even Massachusetts looked to Missouri to help fill up an African American regiment in 1863. By the end of the war, 40 percent of able-bodied Black men in Missouri had joined the Union army.[362]

Enslaved people who ran away to join the army in Missouri often put their families at risk, however. Their jilted masters might abuse the wife or children left behind or put them up for sale in Kentucky, where slavery was still a protected institution. However, even General John Schofield, who was generally sympathetic to the interests of slaveholders, banned the removal of slaves from the state in Special Order 307 issued in November 1863, as such removals interfered with army recruitment.[363]

African American and white soldiers were housed close together, but in separate quarters. There were separate wards for Black and white soldiers in the hospital. Even before that, however, there were African American refugees in the camp looking for work. White soldiers had varied reactions

The former site of Camp Benton is part of Fairground Park in north St. Louis. *Peter Downs.*

to being around African Americans. Edward Hartley was so taken with sympathy for refugees who flooded the camp that he pledged to do everything in his power to defend them against any attempt to re-enslave them.[364] Joseph Fardell, however, was outraged at having to share a chapel with African American soldiers.[365]

Nonetheless, the shared space and experiences began to chip away at some segregationist practices in St. Louis. In one recorded case, eleven white soldiers and an officer left a streetcar in protest when the conductor insisted that a Black soldier could not ride inside the car.[366] In another case, leading white Unionists supported Meachum and the Colored Ladies' Union Aid Society when they sought to ride streetcars to Benton Barracks to provide nursing care in the Black wards or work with refugees. A compromise allowed them to ride inside streetcars on Saturdays.[367] Gratz Brown was president of one of the streetcar companies.

HYDE PARK

Recruits training at Benton Barracks often went to nearby Hyde Park to relax at the beer garden there. On hot evenings, there was no better place to be.

Soldiers and neighborhood residents thronged to the park for Independence Day festivities on July 4, 1863. The day promised music, rides in the gondola of a hot-air balloon and fireworks. Not everything worked as promised, however. Hundreds of people lined up impatiently with tickets for the balloon ride. Some young men pulled down part of the encircling fence so they could cut to the front of the line, which set off much pushing and shoving. A provost marshal and a few soldiers from the Second Regiment, Military Light Artillery, restored order.

Later, a disturbance broke out at the beer garden operated by a Mr. Kuhlage. The *Missouri Democrat* reported that soldiers from the Benton Barracks didn't like Kuhlage. They called him a secessionist because he cut off service to soldiers who wouldn't pay for their drinks.[368]

Many in the crowd at the beer garden had become quite drunk by midafternoon. Kuhlage reportedly told the bartenders to stop selling beer, but a fight broke out when a soldier complained and tried to serve himself. A bartender pulled a knife and slashed the soldier's arm. That ignited a full-scale brawl. People's reactions varied: some proceeded to loot the bar's cellar; others ran for the gates to escape. Police, with the assistance of sober soldiers from the Second, restored order temporarily.

Soldiers from Benton Barracks often went to Hyde Park to relax and drink. Park photo by Emil Boehl. *Missouri Historical Society.*

Back in the line for balloon rides, the balloon operators were having trouble keeping the craft inflated. At around 5:00 p.m., part of the crowd stormed the balloon's staging area. They knocked over the stove that heated the balloon air, probably inadvertently. Flames from the stove set the balloon on fire and then spread to the fireworks. The explosion of fireworks sent some people hurrying home.

Meanwhile, an angry mob composed mainly of Benton Barracks recruits headed for Kuhlage's home. Kuhlage, however, had already run to Fort Number 10 for help. The fort was manned by local men from the Second Regiment, most of them German like Kuhlage.

Fort Number 10 was immediately east of Hyde Park. The trapezoid-shaped fort, up to four hundred feet on a side and surrounded by a three-foot-deep trench, was designed for forty men.[369] The lieutenant on duty answered Kuhlage's plea for help with twenty men. They tried unsuccessfully to block the mob. Witnesses said later that they heard the lieutenant order his men to fire blanks over the heads of the mob as a warning to stop. Some of the soldiers mistakenly loaded live ammunition into their muskets and fired too low. Four soldiers from Benton Barracks and two civilians were killed. Several other people were wounded.[370]

A coroner's jury determined that the soldiers had fired on the crowd without sufficient cause and called for those responsible for the deaths to be identified and tried for murder. The community rallied around the soldiers, however. Two reviews were made of the fifty-seven men assigned to the fort, but no one made any positive identifications, and no one was prosecuted.[371]

This episode is often described as a Unionist attack on a secessionist, but some drunks are angry drunks, and it is not unusual for them to hurl insults when someone tries to stop their drinking. This clash may have been more about tensions between locals and out-of-towners than about stances on secession. After all, there were Union soldiers on both sides, and the local ones backed up the bar owner.

PART IV

BLAIR AND
ST. LOUIS GENERALS

ULYSSES S GRANT

U lysses S Grant was the most successful of the generals connected to St. Louis and possibly the only one without a close connection to Frank Blair. The Ulysses S Grant National Historic Site, 7400 Grant Road, memorializes a personal part of Grant's life but not his military or political accomplishments. It is more closely associated with his in-laws, the Dents, than it is with Grant himself. It was the farm his father-in-law banished him from when Ulysses expressed his desire to join the Union side in the Civil War.[372]

Grant emerged as the Civil War's preeminent general. He won the war in the West, taking control of the Mississippi River and then striking eastward to carve up the Confederacy. Taking command in the East, he did what five predecessors could not do. He contained and defeated Robert E. Lee and did it while overseeing the strategy of slicing up and defeating the South.

He didn't start out with the connections to be a general. He sought an officer's commission from Frank Blair, who was enrolling the volunteers Lincoln requested from Missouri, since the governor wouldn't do it. But Grant got nowhere.[373] Most of the soldiers recruited in the early days of the war were in state units. It was common then for politicians to arrange commissions for would-be officers, who would be in debt to the politician who gave them their starts. If they did well, the soldiers would reflect well on that politician.[374] Grant found a patron in Illinois.

Ten months after Camp Jackson, Frank Blair's friends, including Secretary of War Simon Cameron, Missouri's two U.S. senators and four of Missouri's

Right: General Grant's statue is in front of City Hall at Twelfth and Market on Henri Chouteau's former homesite. *Peter Downs*.

Below: White Haven was Julia Dent Grant's family's plantation. Photo by Carol M. Highsmith. *Library of Congress*.

congressmen, pressured Lincoln to make Blair commander of the Mississippi River campaign in place of Grant. Lincoln demurred, saying, "A man was better qualified to do a thing because he had learned how," and Frank hadn't learned.[375] Instead, Blair ended up in Grant's army.

Grant was not the kind of person Blair would have thought well of before the war. He had failed as a farmer and a businessman. For a while, he sold firewood in St. Louis from trees he cut on his farm. He'd bring it by wagon down Gravois Road, making deliveries to Taylor Blow and others. He used to stop at a saloon and store on the corner of Victor and Gravois to water his horse and buy lunch or coffee and sugar for home.[376]

Grant lived at seven places in St. Louis. Besides White Haven, which is part of the Ulysses S Grant National Historic Site, there was the house he had built on his farm. He called the house Hardscrabble.[377] That house has been moved several times and is now part of Grant's Farm.

Grant lived at two locations in Soulard. One, at the southeast corner of Lynch and Seventh Streets,[378] is now a parking lot for Anheuser-Busch. The other was at 1008 Barton Street. Grant swapped his farm for the two-story house on an otherwise vacant block and a $3,000 promissory note.[379] The private house now at the site is not the same house, contrary to the claims of some historians. Not only is the size and orientation different, but also the foundation is made of concrete block, which wasn't produced commercially until 1900.[380]

Grant also tried his hand as a rental agent, but he failed at collecting rents.[381] That business, Boggs & Grant, shared on office with a law firm on the north side of Pine Street, just east of Third Street.[382] That location is now under the Gateway Arch park.

One thing Grant excelled at was math. He studied for years for a professorship[383] but ended up not applying for an open position at Washington University, because he believed other applicants were more qualified.[384]

Grant showed few hints of military genius in his time in St. Louis, but he did flash signs of the humanity that would lead him to try unsuccessfully to win the country to a vision of a multiracial nation after the war. Unlike his father-in-law, who supervised enslaved people from horseback and whipped any who disobeyed, Grant worked alongside enslaved people doing the work with them and was known for not using a whip.[385] He sometimes hired free African American laborers and paid them the same rate white workers got, which upset his neighbors.[386]

He freed the only person he enslaved, thirty-five-year-old William Jones, in March 1859, when he could have sold him or required Jones to purchase

Ulysses Grant built a cabin for his family in 1855 and '56 with the help of neighbors and hired enslaved people. Photo by Lester Jones (1940). *Library of Congress.*

his freedom. Grant had acquired Jones from his father-in-law within the previous few months.[387] Historian Ron Chernow speculates that Dent had given Jones to Grant as a gift.[388] Rumors that the state legislature was going to make it illegal or very expensive to free an enslaved person prompted moderate abolitionists like Frank Blair to free their slaves around that time, but the quickness with which Grant freed Jones after acquiring him suggests to Chernow that Grant never intended to live as someone who enslaved others.[389]

Grant acquired White Haven from the Dents after the Civil War. (Dent failed as a farmer when he didn't have enslaved people to do the work.) Grant's dream was to retire there and raise horses.[390] He transferred ownership of the property to pay off debts after he was defrauded of his life savings.[391]

Historian William Winter states that St. Louis has not done much to remember Grant.[392] Judge John A. Terry, president of the Missouri Historical Society, lamented the same in 1902 when urging the federal government to buy the Dent farm and make it a national park.

Grant's Barton Street home survived into the mid-twentieth century. Photo by William G. Swekosky (1949). *Missouri Historical Society.*

A privately owned modest twentieth-century home occupies the site at 1008 Barton, where Grant's two-room house had been. *Peter Downs.*

"What will our foreign visitors think of us for not preserving the home of our greatest general, U.S. Grant?," he asked.[393] Ironically, the farm was preserved by a former Confederate officer who married into the extended Bates-Gamble family. It would be another eighty-seven years before the U.S. government bought the property. Judge Henry Sutton, described as a neighbor of the Dents, opposed Terry's plea on the grounds that the work that made Grant famous was done after he left St. Louis.[394]

One element of the city's cold shoulder to Grant's memory undoubtedly was political. Frank Blair reemerged after the war as a power in the Missouri Democratic Party, and he vociferously opposed Grant and his policy of racial equality.[395] His cousin Governor B. Gratz Brown, was one of the leaders of the split in the Missouri Republican Party that created the Independent Republicans, who worked with the Democrats in opposition to Grant and racial equality.[396]

29

WILLIAM T. SHERMAN

rank Blair had a very different attitude toward William Sherman than
he did toward Ulysses Grant, both at the start of the war and at the
end. Although he turned a cold shoulder to Grant's effort to join the
Union war effort, he courted Sherman.

Sherman moved to St. Louis on March 27, 1861, after resigning as
superintendent of the Louisiana State Seminary of Learning and Military
Academy rather than provide space to store weapons seized from the U.S.
Arsenal at Baton Rouge.[397] He came to St. Louis to take up the presidency
of the St. Louis Railroad Company.[398] That company operated horse-drawn
streetcars on Fifth Street[399] (now Broadway). It was Sherman's fourth job
in four years, despite (or because of) his powerful family connections. His
father-in-law was a former senator and former cabinet secretary, and his
brother John was a senator.

Sherman, his wife, five children and two servants moved into a three-
story brick house on Locust Street between Tenth and Eleventh Streets. His
brother-in-law and a friend moved in as boarders to help pay the rent.[400]

Sherman hadn't been in the job long when he received a telegram from
Montgomery Blair offering him the job of chief clerk in the War Department
with a promise of becoming assistant secretary of war.[401] Sherman didn't
seem to question how the postmaster general could offer him a job under
another cabinet secretary, perhaps because he understood how the patronage
system worked. Cabinet secretaries recommended people to one another
for jobs and traded favors, and as postmaster general, Montgomery Blair

General William Sherman bought this house at 912 North Garrison with a cash gift he received from a committee of St. Louisans. *Missouri Historical Society.*

had a lot of favors to trade. Sherman knew something of that secondhand: his father-in-law had been the first secretary of the interior and replaced everyone transferred over to his new department with new patronage employees. Sherman knew the Blairs controlled a lot of patronage jobs, and he didn't like it.[402]

Sherman turned down the job, perhaps because he had recently met with Lincoln at his brother's request and came away from the meeting frustrated that Lincoln did not seem to take the threat of war seriously.[403]

Frank Blair contacted Sherman again a couple of weeks later, after the fall of Fort Sumter in South Carolina, and offered him General Harney's job and the rank of brigadier general of volunteers. Sherman turned that down, too, writing angrily to his brother that Frank "wants to make use of me."[404] Shortly thereafter, he wrote to the secretary of war to say that he was unwilling to take the position as a three-month volunteer, because it would be too disruptive for his family, but that he would be happy to serve as a three-year volunteer.[405]

Sherman got a telegraph from his brother John on May 14, 1861, telling him he'd been appointed colonel in a newly authorized regiment of the regular army. After setting his affairs in order, Sherman went off to Washington.[406] He returned to St. Louis in late August with the rank of brigadier general to ask General Frémont about the availability of troops to serve in Kentucky in the Army of the Cumberland, of which he was second in command.[407] He stayed at the Planter's House.

In October, Sherman found himself in command of the Army of the Cumberland.[408] He, like Frémont in Missouri, exaggerated the strength of the enemy more and more. Secretary of War Simon Cameron stopped in Louisville, Kentucky, on his way to St. Louis to investigate General Frémont. He was so astonished by Sherman's anxieties and exaggerations that he told reporters Sherman was "absolutely crazy."[409]

Sherman was removed from command in mid-November and sent back to St. Louis to report to General Henry Halleck. Halleck sent him to inspect troops in Sedalia, where things were quiet, but Sherman was so afraid of an attack that he ordered the troops stationed in the area to concentrate in one spot. Halleck recalled him, ordered him to go home to his family for twenty days and wrote to Washington that Sherman was "unfit for duty."[410]

Halleck put the disgraced Sherman in charge of training new recruits at Benton Barracks on Sherman's return to St. Louis.[411] It wouldn't be a permanent demotion, however. Sherman benefited from having influential family and friends. Halleck knew that Sherman's brother and father-in-law, as well as their friend Treasury Secretary Salmon Chase, were lobbying

General Sherman is buried with his family at Calvary Cemetery, 5239 West Florissant Avenue. *Peter Downs.*

on Sherman's behalf. After Grant captured Fort Henry on the Ohio River in February 1862 and then moved against Fort Donelson, Halleck sent Sherman to Paducah to assist Grant with more men and supplies.[412] Sherman's willingness to support Grant even though Grant was the junior officer set the stage for the partnership that would win the war.

Frank Blair was assigned with several newly recruited brigades from St. Louis to Sherman in the Mississippi campaign. Blair and Sherman initially detested each other when they finally had the experience of working together. Blair blamed Sherman for the Union's failure to take the bluffs at Chickasaw Bayou and for the heavy casualties his brigades took in the assault. Sherman blamed Blair for blabbing to reporters.[413] The two eventually became friends, however, and Blair would end up joining Sherman's staff.

Four months after the end of the war, a committee of influential St. Louisans gave Sherman $30,000 (equivalent in 2020 to about $500,000) to buy a house in the city. He and his wife bought one at 912 North Garrison Avenue near Franklin Avenue. The family lived there off and on for the next twenty years.[414]

Sherman became estranged from Grant after the war over civil rights for African Americans.[415] Sherman romanticized the South and believed white men should rule. He never understood Grant's support for equal rights for Blacks and whites.

JOHN S. BOWEN

John S. Bowen was General Daniel Frost's second in command in the Missouri Volunteer Militia at Camp Jackson. He took off to join the Confederate army immediately after he pledged not to take up arms against the U.S. government and was released by his Union captors.

Blair and Bowen probably knew each other before the Civil War, politically if not personally. Bowen got active in the Missouri Democratic Party after moving to St. Louis in 1857. Blair was an active Republican and ran for a congressional seat from St. Louis in 1858.

Bowen set himself up as an engineer and architect with an office on Pine Street between Third and Fourth Streets,[416] just one block from Grant's office when the latter worked as a real estate agent.

Bowen and Grant knew each other and apparently got on fairly well.[417] They may have swapped tales of West Point, Jefferson Barracks and marriage. Both men married St. Louis women they met while they were stationed at Jefferson Barracks. Both of them resigned from the army from loneliness after being separated from their wives by army duty.

Bowen was one of the twelve founders of the St. Louis Architects' Association in 1858. He lived with his family in a boardinghouse on Fifth Street (now Broadway) between Chestnut and Pine while he designed and built a house on the heights in Carondelet on land purchased from Henry Blow.[418] That house, with the present address of 6727 Michigan Avenue, still exists but sits vacant and is badly deteriorated.

The house that John Bowen designed and built for his family before the Civil War now sits abandoned and deteriorating. *Peter Downs*.

Bowen was in the political minority in Carondelet. Republicans captured six of eight city council seats in the 1859 election,[419] and many of Bowen's fellow citizens joined the side of the Union. The Carlins, who rented out the house at 122 Davis Street, for example, lost two sons in the Civil War. Attorney General Bates once secured Mrs. Carlin a government escort to Louisiana on a mission to free her son James, who was in a Confederate prison.[420] The Carlins sold the house in 1863 to Conrad Fink, a steamboat captain who carried the U.S. mail between Memphis and St. Louis during the war. Fink later sold it to John Krauss, a former blacksmith at the Iron Mountain Railroad who joined the Union army and bought his own blacksmith shop when he returned from the war.[421]

The nearby Sisters of St. Joseph of Carondelet (6400 Minnesota Avenue) ran a school for African American children and adults until forced to close by state harassment. There is a legend that a hidden room reachable only by a trapdoor in one of the parlors in the convent was a hiding place for people seeking freedom on their journey out of the state.[422] The trapdoor was so effectively disguised that many sisters did not know about it until it was rediscovered during an early-twenty-first-century renovation.[423]

Bowen was the officer Frost entrusted to ask Lyon if he intended to attack. Bowen commanded the Second Regiment of the Missouri

A secret room in the convent of the Sisters of St. Joseph of Carondelet is said to have served as a stop on the Underground Railroad. *Peter Downs.*

Volunteer Milita, which contained the guard's most ardent secessionists,[424] including several companies of Basil Duke's Minute Men,[425] who had joined the militia specifically to counter Blair. Bowen likely would have faced Blair when he rode to the arsenal to deliver Frost's message to Lyon and would have been his prisoner when he was marched out of Camp Jackson between columns of Blair's regiment.

Bowen organized the first unit of Missourians formally enrolled to fight for the South. That unit became the First Missouri Infantry Regiment, CSA.[426]

Bowen and his Missouri regiment faced Blair and his Missourians again at the Siege of Vicksburg, by which time both were generals. Bowen's Missourians fought in three of the five battles the Confederates lost as Grant put a ring around Vicksburg.[427] Blair's men tried to break through the first Missouri Confederates' line on May 22 but were driven back. Bowen's and Blair's men faced each other directly during the ensuing siege, separated by distances of fifty to six hundred yards. The two sides suffered similar losses: 101 killed and 517 wounded among the Missourians on the Union side, and 113 killed and 446 wounded among the Missourians on the Confederate side.[428]

Lookouts in the convent of the Sisters of St. Joseph of Carondelet could tell when the way to the Mississippi River was clear. *Peter Downs*.

The Confederate commanding general at Vicksburg, John Pemberton, sent Bowen to ask Grant for terms of surrender, possibly hoping to play on the past friendship between the two. Grant refused to see him, but his staff made arrangements for Pemberton to meet Grant.[429]

At least some Missouri officers objected to releasing Bowen on parole with the other Confederate combatants captured at Vicksburg, as he had immediately violated the terms of the parole after Camp Jackson. Grant, however, recognized that Bowen was deathly ill. He let Bowen leave in an army ambulance with his wife. Bowen died of dysentery nine days later.[430]

WILLIAM HARNEY

Harney had a reputation in the African American community as the worst kind of enslaver. William Wells Brown, who had escaped from slavery in St. Louis, used him as an example of how barbaric slavery was in Missouri.[431]

Harney beat an enslaved woman named Hannah to death while he served in the U.S. Army as a major at Jefferson Barracks. Other white men in St. Louis, including the city's first mayor, had whipped enslaved women to death without penalty,[432] but Harney was so brutal that he shocked even St. Louis residents. Harney beat Hannah for three successive days in June 1834. He had misplaced some keys and thought she had hidden them, so he beat her repeatedly in a futile effort to get her to confess what she did not know. A coroner's jury viewed the body, listened to testimony from several doctors and recommended he be charged for her death.

An article in the *Cincinnati Journal* labeled Harney "A Monster." The article cited unnamed members of the coroner's jury as stating that the murder was committed "under circumstances of peculiar barbarity" and that Hannah's corpse "exhibited a most shocking sight."[433]

When the details of Hannah's beating got out, an enraged mob gathered to look for Harney, but he had already fled the city, helped by his in-laws, including the future judge and mayor of St. Louis Bryan Mullanphy.[434] He later returned to St. Louis, possibly at the direction of his military superiors. His lawyer got the case moved to Cape Girardeau, and he was acquitted of all charges. The incident hampered neither his military career nor his welcome in elite white society in St. Louis.

The Campbell House Museum at 1508 Locust is the last remaining house from Lucas Place. General William Harney's was near it but east of Fifteenth Street. *Peter Downs*.

Frank Blair may not have cared about the murder, but Harney's close friendships with wealthy supporters of the South and his prejudice against German immigrants surely gave Blair reason to keep an eye on him. Harney hobnobbed with the city's social elite, many of whom favored secession.[435] His very wealthy wife, Mary Mullanphy, did not associate with "low" people.[436] He also was related by marriage to Frost.[437] Like many people in his social circle, he believed the best way to maintain peace in St. Louis was to keep the Germans in check and do nothing to alarm respectable citizens.[438]

Harney's repeated interference in efforts to protect the arsenal soon justified that watch. Schofield concluded that although Harney was, "from his own point of view, thoroughly loyal to the Union," his Union principles were not "up to the standard required by the situation."[439]

Frank Blair sent his brother-in-law Frank Dick to Washington with a report on Harney. Dick arrived in Washington on May 16 and promptly visited Montgomery Blair, who took him to see Secretary of War Simon Cameron. Cameron agreed with their proposal to remove Harney and promote Nathaniel Lyon. They then went to Adjutant General Lorenzo Thomas and got an order on May 18 putting Harney on leave. Lincoln agreed to the order but wrote Frank Blair to use it only when necessary. Frank used it on May 30.[440]

Harney returned to his home on the southeast corner of Lucas Place and Fifteenth Street and spent the rest of the war in retirement. His neighbors on his block included Trusten Polk, who left to serve the Confederacy as a colonel and then a as military judge. The only house left of what had been Lucas Place is the Campbell House, west of Fifteenth Street.

32

JOHN FRÉMONT

The Blairs had lobbied for Frémont's appointment to general in command of the West.[441] It seemed to make sense for personal, political and leadership reasons.

The Blairs and Frémonts were close, personally. Frémont was married to Jessie Benton, daughter of former Missouri senator Thomas Hart Benton, who had been a close political ally of the elder Blair. Jessie and her children had lived at the Blair family estate in Maryland while Frémont was in Washington, D.C., or out west marking possible routes for railroads.[442] The elder Francis Blair championed Frémont's nomination to be the Republican Party's first candidate for president of the United States in 1856 and presided over the convention that made that choice. The Frémonts named their last child after him.[443]

The Benton name was still revered in Unionist circles in St. Louis and Missouri. Jessie had been trained in politics by her father and knew most of the leading players in the Unionist coalition. She was Frémont's closest confidant. She could help him navigate the swirl of political jealousies, factions and coalitions in the state.

Frémont was also revered by the Unionist German community, which was a major part of the Unionist coalition in Missouri and other northwestern states. Thousands of German voters abandoned the Democratic Party in the 1856 election to vote for Frémont. Turner Societies and popular leaders like Franz Sigel backed Frémont because of his support for immigrants and opposition to slavery. The Republicans weren't on the ballot in Missouri in

John and Jessie Frémont rented the Brant house to serve as his residence and headquarters in St. Louis. *Missouri Historical Society.*

1856, but St. Louis Germans followed the campaign in the press and learned the campaign slogan, "Free Speech, Free Press, Free Soil, Free Work, Free Kansas, Frémont!"[444]

Frémont also had a reputation as a can-do kind of guy. His exploits exploring the West had made him famous (thanks to Jessie ghostwriting his accounts). He was the "Pathfinder." He had organized expeditions across the Rockies and overcome everything nature had thrown at him. He was "upright, brave, generous, enterprising, learned and eminently practical."[445]

There were negative sides to his accomplishments that quickly came to the fore, however. He had very little experience of command or of combat. As an explorer, he ran his own show, but without command responsibility. His one experience with command and combat was as leader of a small force in California that took on isolated police garrisons in the war with Mexico. Even then, he disobeyed orders and faced court-martial for insubordination. He was saved only by the strenuous intervention of Jessie's father. He chose to resign from the army, however, rather than work in an organization that questioned his actions.[446]

Frémont's adventures made for good stories and popular reading, but his unwillingness to heed expert advice from trappers and Native American guides got many of his men killed.

Frémont was in France when he learned of the appointment, and it took him nearly two months to reach St. Louis to take up his post. He arrived with a personal bodyguard of three hundred men; their average height was five feet, eleven and a half inches.[447] Despite Jessie's ties to the city, the Frémonts viewed St. Louis as hostile,[448] "a rebel city of a rebel state."[449]

Frémont made his headquarters at the Brant mansion on the southwest corner of Eighth Street and Chouteau Avenue. The site is now part of the Purina campus. The house was owned by Sarah Benton Brant, a relative of Frémont's wife, Jessie Benton,[450] who had hosted the Benton family at their downtown home whenever the senator returned to St. Louis from Washington.[451] The mansion at Eighth and Chouteau was new, having been built in 1859.[452]

It was a controversial choice for a headquarters site. The three-story house had a reputation for opulence, and the rent, $6,000 a year[453] (about $200,000 in 2020), seemed shockingly high, especially to privates, who got paid only $156 a year.[454] Jessie probably made the arrangements. She defended the choice by saying the mansion was "strongly built and fireproof"

A Purina office building occupies the former site of the Brant house. *Peter Downs.*

and convenient for reviewing the regiments.[455] The walled grounds provided additional security.

Frémont converted the basement into an armory and installed staff officers, a printing press and a telegraph office on the first floor. The Frémonts and their closest advisers took up residence on the second and third floors. Guards in the hallways and outside the grounds kept out unwanted visitors, including the new Unionist governor, Hamilton Gamble.[456] Grant later recalled that Frémont acted like a sovereign sitting "in full uniform with his maps before him."[457]

Sherman noted that the people around Frémont could be described as California businessmen of questionable ethics. One of them had just been awarded the contract to build forts around St. Louis. Two of them were failed bankers rumored to have mishandled their banks' funds. Sherman thought of the saying, "Where the vultures are, there is a carcass close by."[458]

Frémont's habit of thinking rules didn't apply to him had come back. He was entering into contracts without getting authorization or approval from the War Department in Washington.

Frémont made control of the Mississippi and Ohio Rivers his strategic priority.[459] Elaborating on Scott's Anaconda Plan, Frémont aimed to bisect the Confederacy by taking control of the Mississippi River and then use the Cumberland and Tennessee to strike into Tennessee, Alabama and Mississippi.[460] He proposed to do so, however, by marching his army though Missouri and Arkansas to the Arkansas River and thence to the Mississippi.[461]

Lyon, who was short on rations, outnumbered two to one in Springfield and losing men every day because their three-month enlistments were up, requested reinforcements. Frémont ordered him to retreat.[462] Lyon subsequently chose to attack instead and was killed in battle at Wilson's Creek.

Frémont panicked after Wilson's Creek. He moved troops into Lafayette Park and ordered the construction of a ring of forts to protect the city, all while bemoaning what he said was his lack of troops and demanding Washington send him reinforcements. He went outside the chain of command and wired Lincoln directly demanding an answer,[463] much like a panicked Sherman would later do in Kentucky. He subsequently did nothing to stop Price's advance into central and then western Missouri and waited too long to send reinforcements, which might have stopped Price's victory at Lexington, Missouri.

Meanwhile, he froze out both Frank Blair and Gamble. The two had been on opposite sides in the Harney-Lyon tussle, but each found Frémont to be

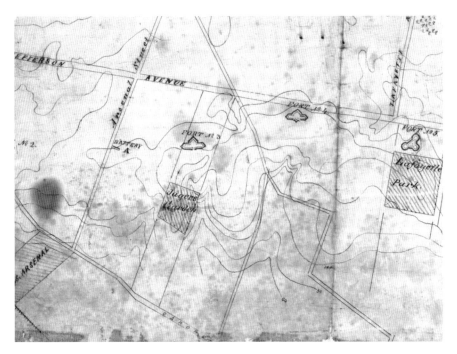

A Civil War military map shows the locations of the arsenal, Jaeger's Garden and Lafayette Park, as well as some of the forts General Frémont ordered built to protect the city. *Missouri Historical Society.*

arrogantly incompetent. Gamble complained to his brother-in-law, Attorney General Bates, and Frank Blair complained to his brother, Postmaster General Montgomery Blair, and those two complained to Lincoln.

Frémont declared martial law after the defeat at Wilson's Creek. The declaration provided for the summary execution of anyone who took up arms against the United States and the emancipation of anyone they had enslaved. Apparently, the only person he consulted about it was Jessie.[464] He didn't even tell Lincoln.

Lincoln learned about the order from newspapers and was appalled.[465] The general had usurped the political power of the president and threatened sensitive negotiations to keep Kentucky and Maryland in the Union. Lincoln asked Frémont to revise the declaration to bring it into line with the Confiscation Act passed by Congress and to avoid antagonizing the people of Kentucky,[466] but Frémont refused. To do so would be tantamount to admitting a mistake. He told Lincoln to order him to make the changes if he really wanted them.[467]

Frank Blair surprised Lincoln by writing that he supported the idea of an emancipation proclamation, but not the timing of it. He said it should be issued when one is winning and it looks as though one can enforce it, not after a defeat and retreat, when it is a dead letter.

Jessie hurried to Washington to instruct Lincoln on the "realities" of the situation and how the emancipation order would keep European powers from siding with the South. Lincoln condescendingly called her "quite a female politician," but he was infuriated by her lecturing tone and subtle threats.[468] He accepted that he would have to bear the brunt of any political blowback from Radical Republicans and turned his private request into a public order.

An angry Francis Blair Sr. later visited Jessie in her hotel room. He revealed that Frank had written a letter critical of Frémont to his brother Monty and that Lincoln was now going to send Monty to St. Louis to examine Frémont's conduct. Jessie replied that Frémont would hold Frank personally responsible.[469] Governor Gamble had delivered one of Frank's letters, along with letters from other leading Unionists critical of Frémont, during a recent

The Marine Hospital cared for wounded in the Civil War and anchored an end of Frémont's line of protective forts. The site was later demolished for construction of a records center of the National Archives. Photo by Emil Boehl. *Missouri Historical Society.*

visit to Washington to meet with Lincoln.[470] Jessie demanded of Lincoln that he give her Frank's letter, but he refused.

Frank's brother Montgomery and brother-in-law Montgomery Meigs reported to Lincoln after their inspection of St. Louis that Frémont was not fit to command the Department of the West. Montgomery Blair said that Frémont "seemed stupefied and almost unconscious and is doing absolutely nothing."[471]

Frémont blamed Frank Blair for his troubles and felt personally betrayed. He had gone out of his way to ask Governor Gamble to make Frank a brigadier general in the Missouri State Guard.[472] The day after the two Montgomerys left St. Louis, Frémont arrested Frank and detained him at the arsenal.[473] The *Missouri Democrat* and German-language newspapers rallied around Frémont, much to Frank's dismay,[474] while the provost marshal general shut down newspapers that supported Frank.[475]

Frémont had a chance to save his position by taking decisive action in the field, but he didn't take it. He was removed from command on November 2, his one-hundredth day. The War Department had set the stage two days before by releasing to the press a scathing report from Adjutant General Lorenzo Thomas that detailed "confusion and imbecility" in Frémont's

An interpretative marker on the west side of Lafayette Park describes the park's place in Civil War St. Louis. *Peter Downs*.

army and concluded that Frémont was "wholly incompetent."[476] Lincoln could use the press just as well as Frémont.

Newspapers greeted Frémont's removal from command as fully justified.[477] The German Americans in his army still admired Frémont, however, and there was fear they would mutiny.[478] They didn't, but the incident raised doubts about Lincoln, the War Department and the leadership of the war. German Americans in St. Louis never again volunteered for service in large numbers.

Frémont returned to St. Louis, where he gave a short speech to his supporters in which he denounced Lincoln as "weak" and an "imbecile."[479]

Frémont's provost marshal general, Major Justus McKinstry, also was his chief quartermaster. That, on top of Frémont's penchant for approving contracts without oversight from Washington, opened up opportunities for demanding kickbacks on military contracts without fear of being investigated. The temptation proved too great. After Frémont was removed from command, McKinstry was arrested, court-martialed and convicted of selling military contracts.[480]

Frémont moved to New York, but he wasn't completely done with St. Louis. B. Gratz Brown and other Radical Republicans backed Frémont for president in 1864 in a challenge to Lincoln from the left. The campaign fizzled, however, when Frémont's most prominent supporters made a deal to support Lincoln in return for Lincoln removing Montgomery Blair from the cabinet.[481]

33

FRANZ SIGEL

Franz Sigel was closely associated with Frank Blair at the start of the Civil War. He turned out to be a thoroughly incompetent general, but he remained popular with the German community and German soldiers and became a symbol for German American participation in the fight to preserve the Union. A statue of Sigel stands in Forest Park on Grand Drive. It was dedicated in 1906 "to remind future generations of the heroism of German-American patriots" in the Civil War.

Sigel was famous in the German immigrant community as the leading general for the liberal revolutions in the Grand Duchy of Baden in 1848 and 1849. He was the general who stayed faithful to republican revolution in Germany when others fled or switched sides. He was known as the military genius who time and time again almost pulled off a victory against vastly superior forces and, when the tide of battle turned against him, saved his armies from destruction by masterful retreats.[482]

Sigel fled Baden after Prussian troops crushed the revolution in 1849, living in exile in Switzerland, France and England before arriving in New York in 1852.[483] He moved to St. Louis in August 1857 to take a professorship at the prestigious Deutsches Institut.[484] He taught math, English, French, German, American history and military tactics.[485] He, his wife and two sons moved into a brick house on Gratiot between Fifth and Sixth Streets, under the shadow of McDowell Medical College. The house site is now part of a highway on-off ramp.

The Franz Sigel monument honors all the German Americans from the St. Louis area who fought for the Union. *Peter Downs*.

Sigel got active in the German community after settling in St. Louis. He taught military tactics to the rifle section of the German Turner Society[486] and wrote articles for the German-language *Westliche Post* and the English-language *Interpreter*.[487] He won a seat on the St. Louis school board in 1860 and tried, unsuccessfully, to introduce bilingual instruction for German students.[488] He traveled the Midwest, campaigning in German immigrant communities in 1860 for Lincoln and Republican candidates.[489]

Sigel was working with Blair to drill Home Guard units in February 1861[490] and accompanied Blair to meetings with Captain Lyon to make plans to defend the U.S. Arsenal in St. Louis.[491] Sigel commanded the Third Regiment, U.S. Volunteers, in Lyon's capture of Camp Jackson and served on Lyon's staff as the general chased the Missouri Volunteer Milita to Springfield.

Historians disagree on whether Lyon should have attacked the much larger Confederate force at Wilson's Creek but agree that Sigel bore much of the responsibility for the fiasco that followed. The Union forces were outnumbered and running low on rations. Frémont ordered Lyon to retreat;[492] Schofield recommended retreat,[493] but Lyon wanted to strike a blow first. He accepted Sigel's plans for a surprise attack that involved dividing his forces to attack from two directions.[494] Sigel, leading the flanking attack, stopped and waited to catch the Confederates in retreat instead of attacking the rear and flank of the army.[495] He got confused, couldn't tell friend from foe and didn't fire on the enemy as they approached to attack him. His men broke and ran in disarray from the shock and confusion of being attacked by troops they expected to be friendly.[496]

The Union forces retreated to Rolla after the battle. The heaviest losses on the Union side were to Frank Blair's regiment, the First Missouri Volunteers. Frank's cousin Cary Gratz was among those killed.[497] Blair was not at the battle. He was still attempting to straddle the military and political worlds. He was in Washington chairing the House Military Affairs Committee[498] after failing to get to elected Speaker of the House.[499]

Sigel took command of the retreat from Springfield to Rolla.[500] Newspapers reported on Sigel's bravery and turned his leadership of the retreat into legend, although the other officers quickly removed him from command and gave leadership of the retreat to another.[501]

The defeat at Wilson's Creek caused General Frémont to order the establishment of a regimental camp in Lafayette Park and the emplacement of two guns and a howitzer at Jaeger's Garden on Tenth Street. He also ordered the construction of a ring of forts around the city, from the Marine Hospital in the south in an arc that ran to Jefferson Avenue in the west to East Grand Avenue in the north.[502]

Sigel resigned from the U.S. Army in protest when command of the army in Missouri was given to General Samuel Curtis instead of him, claiming he was being discriminated against because he was German. He became a rallying figure for German immigrants, who saw his case as representative of the discrimination they endured and of unwarranted suspicions of their patriotism. Sigel Committees sprang up across the country.[503] Soldiers threatened to resign, and mass rallies took place in cities to support Sigel. The controversy even reached the floor of Congress, with one Illinois representative demanding that Sigel be made a major general.[504] Frank Blair, too, lobbied on Sigel's behalf in return for Sigel's support in the 1862 election.[505]

The quandary for Lincoln and the army was that Sigel was too good of a recruiting tool in the German community to leave on the sidelines but too bad of a general to put on the battlefield. Thousands of German men joined the Union army because of their belief in his nobility and military genius.[506] He didn't recognize his own shortcomings, however, and leveraged that devotion for battlefield command. He was transferred to the east and, ultimately, after another embarrassing defeat, was sidelined by General Grant.

JOHN SCHOFIELD

Schofield lived much of the time at the residence of Charles Gibson, opposite Lafayette Park[507] on what is now the southeast corner of Lafayette Avenue and Waverly Place. Gibson was a close confidant of Gamble and Bates. He studied law under Bates and married Gamble's daughter.[508] He was in Washington for most of the war, because Bates had gotten him appointed to the office of solicitor general of the United States. He spent most of his time representing Missouri, however, as the official agent of Gamble's government.[509]

Schofield came to St. Louis in September 1860 to teach physics at Washington University, then on the southwest corner of Washington Avenue and Seventeenth Street. He had taken a one-year leave of absence from the U.S. Army to do so, as there didn't seem to be any prospect for promotion beyond the rank of lieutenant he had held for more than four years.[510]

Schofield reacted to the seizure of federal forts in South Carolina and other Southern states by contacting the War Department to state his readiness to return to service. He received instructions to stay in St. Louis and await orders. After Lincoln called for volunteers to retake federal property on April 15, 1861, the War Department detailed Schofield to muster in the four thousand troops requested from Missouri. He was instructed to contact the governor for the troops. Governor Jackson, however, had already rejected Lincoln's request and did not respond to Schofield's message.[511]

Schofield also contacted General Harney, who would not permit him to enroll any volunteers without a direct order from Washington. Schofield

General John Schofield stayed in Charles Gibson's house opposite Lafayette Park when stationed in St. Louis. This is how the house appeared in 1890. *Missouri Historical Society*.

recalled that Harney downplayed threats to seize the St. Louis Arsenal by stating that Missouri had not passed legislation to secede and was still in the Union.[512]

Lyon and Frank Blair then asked the War Department to give Lyon authority to enroll volunteers. The assistant adjutant general, Major FitzJohn Porter, sent the authorization.[513]

Lyon pulled Schofield out of a church service on April 21 to get ready to muster volunteers into the federal service. Frank Blair made the rounds of German beer gardens, Turner Halls and other Home Guard headquarters to spread the word to Union militiamen to go to the arsenal that night.[514] Schofield spent all night and the next day distributing arms and ammunition and stationing men along the arsenal walls. Only once that was done did he begin the process of formally enrolling the men, organizing them into regiments and supervising the election of officers.[515]

Schofield continued mustering in troops until June 24, six weeks after the Camp Jackson incident, enrolling about fourteen thousand men into the volunteers. The next day, he was assigned at Lyon's request to Lyon's staff as his adjutant general and chief of staff.[516] Schofield defended Lyon's move against Camp Jackson, stating, "Subsequent events showed how illusive was the hope of averting hostilities in any of the border States, and how fortunate it was that active measures were adopted at once."[517]

Schofield took command of the First Missouri, which was Frank Blair's regiment, after the Battle of Wilson's Creek. They were ordered back to St. Louis, where the regiment was converted into an artillery regiment. Blair met Schofield immediately after Schofield arrived in St. Louis and asked him to go with him to see General Frémont in the morning.[518] Schofield expressed a dim view of Frémont after the meeting, "in words rather too strong to repeat in print."[519]

General Halleck appointed Schofield commander of all the militia of Missouri on November 27, 1861, just six days after Schofield's promotion to brigadier general. This militia was the one the new Unionist governor, Hamilton Gamble, raised to defend the state against Confederate attacks. Schofield completed the organization of the militia in April 1862.[520] From then on, Schofield worked closely with Gamble, whose St. Louis home was directly behind the Gibson house where Schofield stayed.

There emerged in 1862 a split in the Unionist camp over the confiscation of property (e.g., enslaved people) of people rebelling against the federal government. Schofield argued that only the judiciary, not the military, could order such confiscations. General Curtis, however, was freeing enslaved people or carrying out, in Schofield's words, "the radical theory of military confiscation."[521]

Gamble opposed the "forced liberation of slaves," and Schofield acted "in harmony with the State government."[522] Rumors swirled of an intended coup, and Blair warned Schofield of a plot to kidnap him and Gamble.[523]

Blair came to Schofield's defense again in August 1862. Henry Blow and three other men went to Washington to urge Lincoln to appoint someone else to command the state militia. Halleck telegraphed Schofield that Frank Blair wanted him removed from command. Schofield showed the message to Blair, who denounced it as false and sent his own telegram back to Halleck disavowing it.[524]

Secretary of War Edwin Stanton wired Schofield an order on September 5, 1862, to enforce the Confiscation Act, and Curtis was assigned to command the new Department of the Missouri.[525] Schofield didn't get along with Curtis. He took sick leave and then got himself transferred to Tennessee.[526]

These condos were built in the early twentieth century on the Gibson homesite. *Peter Downs*.

Schofield was back in St. Louis in May 1863, however, after Lincoln ordered him to replace Curtis in command of the Department of Missouri. Lincoln explained that he didn't think Curtis had done anything wrong, but he had become mired in worsening factionalism in Missouri and opposition to Governor Gamble. The only way to break it up seemed to be to remove either Gamble or Curtis. "As I could not remove Governor Gamble, I had to remove General Curtis," he wrote.[527]

Schofield immediately restricted provost marshals from freeing enslaved people while expressing hope the state convention would approve emancipation. He won Lincoln's gratitude by sending all available forces to assist Grant in taking Vicksburg.

Radicals were unhappy that Schofield pulled back Curtis's policy on emancipations. Charles Drake led a delegation of "Charcoals" (as the radicals were called in Missouri) to Washington to demand that Lincoln remove Schofield, but Lincoln responded with praise for Schofield for freeing up troops for the Vicksburg campaign.[528]

Gamble, who had a close relationship with Schofield, probably was pleased by Schofield's action restricting emancipations, but he wanted more. He wanted a ban on recruiting African Americans into the army and a halt to provost marshals confiscating enslaved people under the Confiscation Act. Schofield refused to agree.[529]

Lincoln sent a letter of support to Schofield in October 1863 that emphasized that the military was neither to return fugitive slaves nor force slaves from their homes and that only Schofield or the War Department had the right to enlist African American troops or confiscate property.[530] A week later, Schofield received an order to raise a regiment of African American volunteers.[531] Lincoln asked Schofield for his assessment of the political factions in Missouri since Blair was away in the army. Schofield insisted that Gamble and his factions were Lincoln's real friends.

Schofield left St. Louis in January 1864 to take command of the Army of the Ohio. He would join up with Frank Blair again in Sherman's march from Atlanta to the sea. Schofield named his charger Frank Blair.[532] Whether that was a sign of fondness or something else is not clear.

NOTES

Chapter 1

1. Newspaper accounts of the time differ on the exact number of enslaved people in the group.
2. "Missouri's Early Slave Laws: A History in Documents."
3. *Missouri Democrat,* May 25, 1855, on microfilm at the St. Louis Public Library Central Library.
4. *Missouri Republican,* May 22, 1855.
5. *Missouri Democrat,* May 23, 1855, p. 3, col. 1.
6. "Missouri's Early Slave Laws: A History in Documents."
7. Roberts, "Crossing Jordan," 33.
8. *Missouri Republican,* May 22, 1855.
9. *Missouri Republican,* July 19, 1855.
10. *Missouri Democrat,* May 23, 1855.
11. Bellamy, "Free Blacks," 211
12. Ibid., 220.
13. Ibid., 219.
14. "Laws of Missouri," 1847, 104.
15. Blackett, *Captive's Quest for Freedom.*
16. *Keemle's St. Louis City Directory for the Years 1836–37.*
17. Hamilton, "Edward Bates and Grape Hill," 3.
18. Bellamy, "Free Blacks," 216.

19. Hamm, "Quaker View," 119. Inflation estimates are from officialdata.org.
20. Ibid., 212, 216.
21. Ibid, 203.
22. John Berry Meachum, "An Address to All the Colored Citizens, St. Louis," 1846, quoted in VanderVelde, *Mrs. Dred Scott*, 225.
23. *Journal of the Missouri State Convention*, 18–19; Bellamy, "Free Blacks," 98.
24. Inflation calculator, officialdata.org
25. Roberts, "Crossing Jordan," 23.
26. "Laws of Missouri, 1843," 208–9; *St. Louis Revised Ordinance, 1835–1836* (St. Louis, Missouri, 1836), 124–26; Bellamy, "Free Blacks," 204–9; Hamm, "A Quaker View," 118.
27. Bellamy, "Free Blacks," 207–8.
28. Bellamy, "Persistency of Colonization in Missouri," 17.
29. Bellamy, "Free Blacks," 208.
30. VanderVelde, *Mrs. Dred Scott*, 224–25.
31. Durst, "Reverend John Berry Meachum, 2.
32. "Laws of Missouri, 1847," 103.
33. Bellamy, "Free Blacks," 224.
34. E.g., Dunst, "Reverend John Berry Meachum."
35. E.g., Roberts, "Crossing Jordan," 37. John and Sylvia Wright call the floating freedom school story a "Baptist legend." Wright and Wright, *Extraordinary Black Missourians*, 27.
36. Hamm, "Quaker View," 119.
37. St. Louis Circuit Court, "St. Louis Mechanics Liens."
38. St. Louis Circuit Court, "Historical Records Project."

Chapter 2

39. Gerteis, *Civil War St. Louis*, 10, 31; VanderVelde, *Mrs. Dred Scott*, 132.
40. Dunson, "Notes on the Missouri Germans on Slavery," 355–59; Gerteis, *Civil War St. Louis*, 7–11; Herman, "McIntosh Affair," 125–26; Laughlin, "Endangering the Peace of Society; Lovejoy, "Awful Murder and Savage Barbarity."
41. Laughlin, "Endangering the Peace," 3.
42. Ibid.
43. Seematter, "Trials and Confessions," 46.
44. Moore, "Ray of Hope, Extinguished," 11.
45. Laughlin, "Endangering the Peace." 5–6.

46. Basler, ed., *The Collected Works of Abraham Lincoln*, v. 1:109–10.
47. Gerteis, *Civil War St. Louis*, 10.
48. VanderVelde, *Mrs. Dred Scott*, 132.
49. Schwarzbach, "Burning of Francis L. McIntosh," 38.
50. Seematter, "Trials and Confessions," 42.
51. Ibid., 45–46.
52. Ibid., 43–44.
53. Ibid., 36–37.
54. Ibid., 46.
55. Bellamy, "Free Blacks," 205–6.
56. Shipley, *History of Black Baptists in Missouri*, 25.

Chapter 3

57. "An Underground Railway Story," *Denver Post*, reprinted in the *Minneapolis Journal*, July 4, 1901, https://www.newspapers.com/clip/3228923/moses-dickson-slave-uprising/. Livingston, "African Life of Resistance"; Wright, *Discovering African American St. Louis*.
58. Dickson, *Manual of the International Order*, 8.
59. Ibid., 9.
60. Ibid., 7.
61. "An Underground Railway Story."
62. Shipley, *History of Black Baptists in Missouri*, 24–5.
63. Dickson, *Manual of the International Order*, 9.
64. "An Underground Railway Story."
65. Dickson, *Manual of the International Order*, 12.

Chapter 4

66. Receipt from bounty hunter Bernard Lynch to Henry Shaw, itemizing costs incurred boarding captive enslaved persons Sarah and Esther. Costs incurred arresting Esther and her subsequent sale to John D. Fondren of Vicksburg for $350. Dated July 30, 1855, *Illustrated History of the Missouri Botanical Garden*.
67. Winter, *Civil War in St. Louis*, 84.
68. Anderson, *Story of a Border City*, 182–86.
69. Ibid., 176.

70. Ibid., 179.
71. Ibid., 180.
72. Eiland, "Unspoken Demand of Slavery," 49–50.

Chapter 5

73. "Awful Murder and Savage Barbarity," *St. Louis Observer*, May 5, 1835.
74. Gerteis, *Civil War St. Louis*, 13; Laughlin, "Endangering the Peace," 5.
75. Gerteis, *Civil War St. Louis*, 13; Laughlin, "Endangering the Peace," 13–14.
76. Gerteis, *Civil War St. Louis*, 14.
77. Ibid.
78. Ibid.
79. Gerteis, *Civil War St. Louis*, 14–15.
80. Ibid; Laughlin, "Endangering the Peace," 14–15.
81. Cain, *Lincoln's Attorney General Edward Bates*, 52.
82. Missouri State Archives, "Missouri's Early Slave Laws."
83. Laughlin, "Endangering the Peace," 9.
84. Hoffman, "If I Fall, My Grave Shall Be in Alton"; Gerteis, *Civil War St. Louis*, 10, 16.
85. Shipley, *History of Black Baptists in Missouri*, 24–25.
86. Laughlin, "Endangering the Peace," 16–17.
87. Ibid., 18.
88. Gerteis, *Civil War St. Louis*, 16.
89. Laughlin, "Endangering the Peace," 19.
90. Ibid.
91. Ibid., 10.
92. Gerteis, *Civil War St. Louis*, 17.
93. Ibid.
94. Laughlin, "Endangering the Peace," 11.

Chapter 6

95. Missouri State Archives, "Before Dred Scott."
96. Ibid.; Gerteis, *Civil War St. Louis*, 18–19; Mason, "Famous for Freedom Suits."
97. "Freedom Suits," Gateway Arch National Park.

98. Delaney, *From the Darkness Cometh the Light*.
99. The case is Polly Wash v. Joseph McMegahan, filed November 20, 1859, "Suits for Freedom, St. Louis, 1804–65." Enslaved people often were given the last name of the enslaver they lived with in legal papers.
100. Moore, "Ray of Hope," 7; VanderVelde, *Mrs. Dred Scott*, 235–36.
101. There are many descriptions of the Scotts' legal arguments for freedom. The three I most rely on here are: VanderVelde, *Mrs. Dred Scott*; Gerteis, *Civil War St. Louis*, 19–29; and "Dred Scott Case, 1846–1857," Missouri State Archives.
102. VanderVelde, *Mrs. Dred Scott*, 233.
103. *Green's St. Louis Business Directory 1847*.
104. Ibid.
105. VanderVelde, *Mrs. Dred Scott*, 394 n. 69.
106. Ibid., 232.
107. Ibid., 222. VanderVelde argues that Harriet lived in the Russells' compound on Fourth Street while she worked for them.
108. VanderVelde, *Mrs. Dred Scott*, 226.
109. Shipley, *History of Black Baptists in Missouri*, 24.
110. Anderson, *Story of a Border City*, 12; "Central Baptist Church Celebrates 170th Anniversary," *St. Louis American*, April 7, 2016.
111. Winter, *Civil War in St. Louis*, 118.
112. Bellamy, "Free Blacks," 221.
113. "Petitions to Leave to Sue for Freedom," Revised Dred Scott Case Collection.
114. Ibid.
115. Hoffman, "If I Fall," 19.
116. Gerteis, *Civil War St. Louis*, 22; VanderVelde, *Mrs. Dred Scott*, 245.
117. VanderVelde, *Mrs. Dred Scott*, 245.
118. Gerteis, *Civil War St. Louis*, 23; VanderVelde, *Mrs. Dred Scott*, 244–46.
119. "Proceedings of the First Day," *New York Times*.
120. VanderVelde, *Mrs. Dred Scott*, 243, writes that Murdoch was driven out of town by former judge Bryan Mullanphy.
121. Ibid., 410, n. 82.
122. "Suits for Freedom, St. Louis, 1804–65."
123. VanderVelde, *Mrs. Dred Scott*, 283.
124. Moore, "Ray of Hope," 4–12.
125. Ibid., 284.
126. VanderVelde, *Mrs. Dred Scott*, 292.
127. Ibid., 292.

Chapter 7

128. VanderVelde, *Mrs. Dred Scott*, 188.
129. Ibid., 189–91.
130. Ibid., 190–91.
131. Ibid., 305.
132. Ibid., 308.
133. Winter, *Civil War in St. Louis*, 98–99.

Chapter 8

134. "This Was St. Louis Slave Market," *St. Louis Star and Times*.
135. Ibid.
136. "Dred Scott Case, 1846–1857," Missouri State Archives.
137. Gerteis, *Civil War St. Louis*, 23–24; VanderVelde, *Mrs. Dred Scott*, 248–51; "Dred Scott Case, 1846–1857," Missouri State Archives.
138. *Kennedy's St. Louis Directory*, 1860, gives Frank Blair's house as Charlotte's residence.
139. "Dred Scott Case, 1846–1857," Missouri State Archives.
140. Ibid.; Gerteis, *Civil War St. Louis*, 63–64.
141. "Dred Scott Case, 1846–1857," Missouri State Archives; VanderVelde, *Mrs. Dred Scott*, 310.
142. Bellamy, "Free Blacks," 206.
143. Basler, *Collected Works of Abraham Lincoln*, 109–10.
144. Foner, *Fiery Trial*, 103–4.

Chapter 9

145. Gerteis, *Civil War St. Louis*, 27.
146. Ibid., 29.
147. Ibid., 64.
148. Chernow, *Grant*, 62.

Chapter 10

149. *Morrison's St. Louis Directory 1852*.
150. As reported in numerous St. Louis city directories from 1845 to 1855.

151. Parrish, *Frank Blair*, 48.
152. Gerteis, *Civil War St. Louis*, 58.
153. Parrish, *Frank Blair*, 51.
154. Goodwin, *Team of Rivals*, 676–79.
155. *Missouri Democrat*, July 12, 1855.
156. Foner, *Fiery Trial*, 124; Goodwin, *Team of Rivals*, 24.
157. Parrish, *Frank Blair*, 74–75.
158. Foner, *Fiery Trial*, 124–30.
159. Foner, *Fiery Trial*, 128; Parrish, *Frank Blair*, 68.
160. Foner, *Fiery Trial*, 127.
161. Gerteis, *Civil War St. Louis*, 70.
162. Peterson, "Political Fluctuations of B. Gratz Brown," 26.
163. Parrish, *Frank Blair*, 80–81.

Chapter 11

164. Cain, *Lincoln's Attorney General Edward Bates*, 46.
165. VanderVelde, *Mrs. Dred Scott*, 280.
166. Cain, *Lincoln's Attorney General Edward Bates*, 59–60.
167. Goodwin, *Team of Rivals*, 25.
168. Ibid., 26; Gerteis, *Civil War St. Louis*, 76.
169. Goodwin, *Team of Rivals*, 248–49.

Chapter 12

170. Forest Park Statues and Monuments.
171. Parrish, *Frank Blair*, 90.
172. Gerteis, *Civil War St. Louis*, 80; Phillips, "Radical Crusade," 26.
173. Gerteis, *Civil War St. Louis*, 82; Phillips, "Radical Crusade," 26.
174. Gerteis, *Civil War St. Louis*, 88; Harding, *Life of George R. Smith*, 313.
175. Gerteis, *Civil War St. Louis*, 81; Phillips, "Radical Crusade," 26; Harding, *Life of George R. Smith*, 313.
176. Rombauer, *Union Cause in St. Louis*, 128.
177. Gerteis, *Civil War St. Louis*, 81.
178. *Kennedy's St. Louis Directory*, 1859.
179. Parrish, *Frank Blair*, 85. The Democratic Party equivalents were known as Constitutional Guards and Broom Rangers.

180. Gerteis, *Civil War St. Louis*, 80.
181. Ibid., 85–89.

Chapter 13

182. Winter, *Civil War in St. Louis*, 31.
183. Duke, *Reminiscences*, 38.
184. Gerteis, *Civil War St. Louis*, 85.
185. Ibid.
186. Duke, *Reminiscences*, 39. Duke consistently referred to the Republican Home Guards as Wide Awakes.
187. Ibid.
188. Duke, *Reminiscences*, 39–40.
189. Ibid., 42.
190. Ibid.
191. Schofield, "Response to Letter from Pierre Berthold."

Chapter 14

192. Gerteis, *Civil War St. Louis*, 25.
193. Gerteis, *Civil War St. Louis*, 67; Harding, *Life of George R. Smith*, 312.
194. Parrish, *Frank Blair*, 93.
195. *Journal and Proceedings of the Missouri State Convention*, 55–58; Harding, *Life of George R. Smith*, 314; Civil War Centennial Commission, *Civil War in Missouri*, 3; Rombauer, *Union Cause in St. Louis*, 171–72.
196. Roe, "Missouri Rejects Secession."

Chapter 15

197. Winter, *Civil War in St. Louis*, 45; Rombauer, *Union Cause in St. Louis*, 431.
198. Rombauer, *Union Cause in St. Louis*, 202.
199. Ibid., 197.
200. Ibid., 200–2.
201. Ibid., 459.
202. Ibid., 473.
203. Cosner and Shannon, *Missouri's Mad Doctor McDowell*, 85.

204. Boernstein, *Memoirs of a Nobody*, 178–82; Ritter, "St. Louis Know-Nothing Riots of 1854," 30.

205. Rombauer, *Union Cause in St. Louis*, 196; Winter, *Civil War in St. Louis*, 45.

Chapter 16

206. Chernow, *Grant*, 134; Duke, *Reminiscences*, 37; Gerteis, *Civil War St. Louis*, 82; Winter, *Civil War in St. Louis*, 38–39.

207. Duke, *Reminiscences*, 37.

208. Floyd, "Dispatch to Major Bell."

209. Gerteis, *Civil War St. Louis*, 83; Phillips, "Radical Crusade," 29.

210. Gerteis, *Civil War St. Louis*, 84.

211. Rombauer, *Union Cause in St. Louis*, 198.

212. McElroy, *Struggle for Missouri*, 37–39; Parrish, *Frank Blair*, 86; Winter, *Civil War in St. Louis*, 39.

213. Gerteis, *Civil War St. Louis*, 85; Winter, *Civil War in St. Louis*, 39.

214. Gerteis, *Civil War St. Louis*, 86; Winter, *Civil War in St. Louis*, 39.

215. Gerteis, *Civil War St. Louis*, 87.

216. Gerteis, *Civil War St. Louis*, 89; Winter, *Civil War in St. Louis*, 39.

217. Wayne, "Establishing a Metropolitan Police Force," 34.

218. Ibid., 35.

219. Gerteis, *Civil War St. Louis*, 92.

220. Ibid., 93–94.

221. Ibid.

222. Gerteis, *Civil War St. Louis*, 93; Wayne, "Establishing a Metropolitan Police Force," 35.

223. Reavis and Clay, *Life and Military Services of Gen. William Selby Harney*, 353; Winter, *Civil War in St. Louis*, 39.

224. Schofield, *Forty-Six Years in the Army*, 71; Gerteis, *Civil War St. Louis*, 93–94; Winter, *Civil War in St. Louis*, 39.

225. Gerteis, *Civil War St. Louis*, 94.

226. Duke, *Reminiscences*, 44–45.

227. Rombauer, *Union Cause in St. Louis*, 196–99.

228. Gerteis, *Civil War St. Louis*, 96.

229. Rombauer, *Union Cause in St. Louis*, 203–5, 417–64.

Chapter 17

230. Gerteis, *Civil War St. Louis*, 98; Parrish, *Frank Blair*, 100.
231. Rombauer, *Union Cause in St. Louis*, 238; Winter, *Civil War in St. Louis*, 40.
232. Parrish, *Frank Blair*, 100.
233. Gerteis, *Civil War St. Louis*, 100; Winter, *Civil War in St. Louis*, 40.
234. McElroy, *Struggle for Missouri*, 72; Gerteis, *Civil War St. Louis*, 100; Parrish, *Frank Blair*, 101; Rombauer, *Union Cause in St. Louis*, 225.
235. Duke, *Reminiscences*, 50–51.
236. Ibid., 51.
237. "G.W. Letter to Dear Brother, Camp Jackson, St. Louis, May 9, 1861."
238. Winter, *Civil War in St. Louis*, 40.
239. Gerteis, *Civil War St. Louis*, 102–3; Winter, *Civil War in St. Louis*, 42.
240. McElroy, *Struggle for Missouri*, 73–74; Winter, *Civil War in St. Louis*, 40–42; Rombauer, *Union Cause in St. Louis*, 231.
241. Gerteis, *Civil War St. Louis*, 106; Reavis and Clay, *Life and Military Services of Gen. William Selby Harney*, 359; Winter, *Civil War in St. Louis*, 48.
242. Gerteis, *Civil War St. Louis*,110; Phillips, "The Radical Crusade," 38.
243. Chernow, *Grant*, 134.

Chapter 18

244. "Camp Jackson Incident," *Museum Gazette*, 1.
245. Gerteis, *Civil War St. Louis*, 107; Winter, *Civil War in St. Louis*, 49.
246. Winter, *Civil War in St. Louis*, 50.
247. Gerteis, *Civil War St. Louis*, 108–9; Rombauer, *Union Cause in St. Louis*, 233–34; Winter, *Civil War in St. Louis*, 50–53.
248. Grissom, "Personal Recollections of Distinguished Missourians," 95.
249. Ibid., 96–97. Many of the city's Virginia-born elite, like Wright, did not think of Germans as citizens.
250. Ibid.
251. Winter, *Civil War in St. Louis*, 140.
252. Paxton, *Annals of Platte County, Missouri*, 284.
253. Ibid., 764.
254. Thompson, *Story of Mattie J. Jackson*, 10–11.
255. Anderson, *Story of a Border City*, 181.
256. Ibid., 204.
257. Winter, *Civil War in St. Louis*, 69–70.

Chapter 19

258. Anderson, *Story of a Border City*, 106.
259. Rombauer, *Union Cause in St. Louis*, 223, 243.
260. Rombauer, *Union Cause in St. Louis*, 223; Winter, *Civil War in St. Louis*, 124.
261. Anderson, *Story of a Border City*, 106–7; Gerteis, *Civil War St. Louis*, 114.
262. Anderson, *Story of a Border City*, 107.

Chapter 20

263. Anderson, *Story of a Border City*, 154.
264. Anderson, *Story of a Border City*, 108; Gerteis, *Civil War St. Louis*, 115.
265. Gerteis, *Civil War St. Louis*, 116.
266. Anderson, *Story of a Border City*, 108–13; Gerteis, *Civil War St. Louis*, 116.
267. Gerteis, *Civil War St. Louis*, 118.
268. Ibid., 118.
269. Ibid., 119.
270. Ibid., 120–21.
271. Ibid., 121.
272. Bartey, *St. Louis Lost*, 33–5.
273. Gerteis, *Civil War St. Louis*, 123–24; Winter, *Civil War in St. Louis*, 68.

Chapter 21

274. Romeo, "Freedwomen in Pursuit of Liberty," 83.
275. Davis, "Contraband Camps in St. Louis," 22.
276. Romeo, "Freedwomen in Pursuit of Liberty," 82.
277. Bloomberg, *Charitable Women*, 85–86; Gerteis, *Civil War St. Louis*, 208.
278. Davis, "Contraband Camps in St. Louis," 25; Romeo, "Freedwomen in Pursuit of Liberty," 45.
279. Davis, "Contraband Camps in St. Louis," 24.

Chapter 22

280. Arenson, *Great Heart of th3e Republic*, 132.
281. Kelly, "MCC Assembly."
282. Faherty, *Exile in Erin*, 38.

283. "Lucas Place in a Nutshell."
284. Ibid., for residents; Winter, *Civil War in St. Louis*, 127, for Polk's political orientation.
285. Faherty, *Exile in Erin*, 20.
286. Ibid., 16.
287. Ibid., 36.
288. Ibid., 39.
289. Ibid., 129.
290. Ibid., 138–39.
291. Arenson, *Great Heart of the Republic*, 132.
292. Ibid., 133.

Chapter 23

293. Gerteis, *Civil War St. Louis*, 170; Winter, *Civil War in St. Louis*, 80.
294. Cosner and Shannon, *Missouri's Mad Doctor McDowell*, 42.
295. Ibid., 85.
296. McDowell, "Letter to Henry Ward Beecher," reprinted in Cosner and Shannon, *Missouri's Mad Doctor McDowell*, 124.
297. Cosner and Shannon, *Missouri's Mad Doctor McDowell*, 88.
298. Ibid., 90.
299. Ibid., 94.
300. Gerteis, *Civil War St. Louis*, 179.
301. Ibid., 171–72.
302. Ibid., 188–89.
303. Ibid., 190.
304. Ibid., 189–94.

Chapter 24

305. Milligan, *Gunboats Down the Mississippi*, xxi–xxii.
306. Flood, *Grant and Sherman*, 188; Milligan, *Gunboats Down the Mississippi*, xxiv.
307. Milligan, *Gunboats Down the Mississippi*, xxiv.
308. Ibid., xix, along with the Ohio River valley.
309. Ibid., xviii.
310. Ibid., xix–xx.

311. Ibid., xxvi.

312. Winter, *Civil War in St. Louis*, 78.

313. Ibid.

314. Gerteis, *Civil War St. Louis*, 239.

315. "City Class Ironclads," Vicksburg National Military Park.

316. Milligan, *Gunboats Down the Mississippi*, 3.

317. Ibid.

318. *Kennedy's St. Louis Directory*, 1860.

319. Milligan, *Gunboats Down the Mississippi*, 4.

320. Ibid., 5.

321. Ibid., 6.

322. Gerteis, *Civil War St. Louis*, 239.

323. Milligan, *Gunboats Down the Mississippi*, 13.

324. Gerteis, *Civil War St. Louis*, 238; Joiner, *Mr. Lincoln's Brown Water Navy*, 23.

325. Milligan, *Gunboats Down the Mississippi*, xxv.

326. Ibid., 16.

327. Gerteis, *Civil War St. Louis*, 240–41.

328. Milligan, *Gunboats Down the Mississippi*, 16.

329. Gerteis, *Civil War St. Louis*, 249.

330. Milligan, *Gunboats Down the Mississippi*, 21.

331. Ibid., 22.

332. Joiner, 144.

333. Gerteis, *Civil War St. Louis*, 249–50.

334. Sneddeker, et al., National Register of Historic Places Nomination Form, Carondelet East of Broadway.

335. Gerteis, *Civil War St. Louis*, 253.

336. Sneddeker, et al., National Register of Historic Places Nomination Form, Carondelet East of Broadway, Item 7: 9.

337. Gerteis, *Civil War St. Louis*, 255–57; Rosecrans, "General Order No. 65."

Chapter 25

338. Chernow, *Grant*, 29.

339. "Historic Jefferson Barracks," Missouri Civil War Museum; Winter, *Civil War in St. Louis*, 5–6.

340. Gerteis, *Civil War St. Louis*, 92.

341. Anderson, *Story of a Border City*, 288–90.

342. Winter, *Civil War in St. Louis*, 7.

343. Anderson, *Story of a Border City*, 291.
344. *St. Louis—Our Civil War Heritage*, 160; Winter, *Civil War in St. Louis*, 7.
345. Winter, *Civil War in St. Louis*, 91.
346. Anderson, *Story of a Border City*, 290.
347. Ibid., 296–97.
348. Ibid., 310.
349. Ibid., 313.
350. Ibid.
351. Winter, *Civil War in St. Louis*, 144.
352. Ibid., 145.
353. Gerteis, *Civil War St. Louis*, 282.
354. Winter, *Civil War in St. Louis*, 145–46.

Chapter 26

355. Winter, *Civil War in St. Louis*, 73.
356. Stillwell, *Story of a Common Soldier*, 26.
357. Ibid.
358. Kiner, *One Year's Soldiering*, 11–12.
359. Romeo, "Freedwomen in Pursuit of Liberty," 93.
360. Winter, *Civil War in St. Louis*, 74.
361. Williams, "U.S. Colored Troops."
362. Gerteis, *Civil War St. Louis*, 291; Romeo, "Freedwomen in Pursuit of Liberty," 93.
363. Romeo, "Freedwomen in Pursuit of Liberty," 85.
364. Hartley, *Letter to Miss Em*.
365. Fardell, *Letter to Father and Mother*.
366. Winter, *Civil War in St. Louis*, 75.
367. Gerteis, *Civil War St. Louis*, 224; Reavis and Clay, *Life and Military Services of Gen. William Selby Harney*, 371.

Chapter 27

368. *Missouri Democrat*, July 6, 1863.
369. "Original plattings of forts at St. Louis, Mo. 186-," Corps of Engineers.
370. *St. Louis Daily Evening News*, July 6, 1863; *Missouri Republican*, July 6, 1863.
371. Winter, *Civil War in St. Louis*, 87; *Missouri Democrat*, July 6–10, 1863.

Chapter 28

372. Chernow, *Grant*, 134.

373. McFeely, *Grant*, 75.

374. Ibid.

375. Parrish, *Frank Blair*, 152.

376. "One of Grant's Lounging Places," *St. Louis Post-Dispatch*.

377. Winter, *Civil War in St. Louis*, 11.

378. Chernow, *Grant*, 105, Winter, *Civil War in St. Louis*, 12; "Grant in St. Louis," *St. Louis Post-Dispatch*.

379. Ibid.

380. Hall, *Early Developmental History of Concrete Block*.

381. Chernow, *Grant*, 104–7; Winter, *Civil War in St. Louis*, 12; "Grant in St. Louis," *St. Louis Post-Dispatch*.

382. "Grant in St. Louis," *St. Louis Post-Dispatch*.

383. Chernow, *Grant*, 29; Winter, *Civil War in St. Louis*, 12.

384. Winter, *Civil War in St. Louis*, 12.

385. Chernow, *Grant*, 101.

386. Chernow, *Grant*, 101; McFeely, *Grant*, 63.

387. McFeely, *Grant*, 62, on Grant borrowing Jones from his father-in-law in 1858.

388. Chernow, *Grant*, 106.

389. Ibid.

390. Chernow, *Grant*, 618; Winter, *Civil War in St. Louis*, 13.

391. Chernow, *Grant*, 924.

392. Winter, *Civil War in St. Louis*, 8.

393. "Homes of Heroes Falling in St. Louis," *St. Louis Post-Dispatch*.

394. Ibid.

395. Chernow, *Grant*, 619–20.

396. Chernow, *Grant*, 740–46.

Chapter 29

397. Flood, *Grant and Sherman*, 37.

398. Winter, *Civil War in St. Louis*, 16.

399. Winter, *Civil War in St. Louis*, 16; Flood, *Grant and Sherman*, 51.

400. Winter, *Civil War in St. Louis*, 16.

401. Ibid.

402. Parrish, *Frank Blair*, 97.
403. Flood, *Grant and Sherman*, 51.
404. Parrish, *Frank Blair*, 98.
405. Winter, *Civil War in St. Louis*, 16.
406. Flood, *Grant and Sherman*, 52.
407. Winter, *Civil War in St. Louis*, 16.
408. Flood, *Grant and Sherman*, 59.
409. Ibid., 67.
410. Flood, *Grant and Sherman*, 71; Winter, *Civil War in St. Louis*, 17.
411. Flood, *Grant and Sherman*, 76; Winter, *Civil War in St. Louis*, 17.
412. Flood, *Grant and Sherman*, 79.
413. Parrish, *Frank Blair*, 160–62.
414. Winter, *Civil War in St. Louis*, 18.
415. Goodwin, *Team of Rivals*, 622, 705–6, 809; McFeely, *Grant*, 252, 259.

Chapter 30

416. Winter, *Civil War in St. Louis*, 22.
417. Ibid., 23.
418. Ibid.
419. Sneddeker, National Register of Historic Places Nomination Form. Carondelet East of Broadway, Item 8: 3.
420. Ibid., Item 7: 11.
421. Ibid., Item 7: 11–12.
422. Westerman, "Congregation Confronts Racism."
423. Johnson, "Founder's Day 2011 in St. Louis."
424. Winter, *Civil War in St. Louis*, 42.
425. Ibid., 49.
426. Ibid., 23.
427. Huling, "Missourians at Vicksburg," 3.
428. Huling, "Missourians at Vicksburg," 7–8.
429. Chernow, *Grant*, 286–87; Flood, 181; McFeeley, *Grant*, 137; Winter, *Civil War in St. Louis*, 23.
430. Winter, *Civil War in St. Louis*, 23.

Chapter 31

431. Brown, *Narrative of William W. Brown*, 27.

432. Frazier, *Slavery and Crime in Missouri*, 135.

433. Frazier, *Slavery and Crime in Missouri*, 137.

434. Ibid., 136.

435. Reavis and Clay, *Life and Military Services of Gen. William Selby Harney*, 351.

436. VanderVelde, *Mrs. Dred Scott*, 276.

437. Faherty, SJ, *Exile in Erin*, 33.

438. Gerteis, *Civil War St. Louis*, 95.

439. Schofield, *Forty-Six Years in the Army*, 72–73.

440. Reavis and Clay, *Life and Military Services of Gen. William Selby Harney*, 374–82; Parrish, *Frank Blair*, 104–6.

Chapter 32

441. Goodwin, *Team of Rivals*, 389.

442. Gerteis, *Civil War St. Louis*, 139.

443. Ibid.

444. Engle, *Yankee Dutchman*, 41.

445. Goodwin, *Team of Rivals*, 389.

446. Flood, *Grant and Sherman*, 61–62.

447. McFeely, *Grant*, 88.

448. "Homes of Heroes Falling in St. Louis Beneath Irreverent Hands."

449. Winter, *Civil War in St. Louis*, 71.

450. Gerteis, *Civil War St. Louis*, 142, says they were cousins, as does Hamilton, "New Picture on Glass," 3; Winter, *Civil War in St. Louis*, 71, says Sarah was Jessie's aunt.

451. Hamilton, 3.

452. Ibid.

453. Gerteis, *Civil War St. Louis*, 142; Winter, *Civil War in St. Louis*, 71.

454. Winter, *Civil War in St. Louis*, 71.

455. Ibid.

456. Gerteis, *Civil War St. Louis*, 142; Goodwin, *Team of Rivals*, 389.

457. Chernow, *Grant*, 144.

458. Flood, *Grant and Sherman*, 65.

459. Rombauer, *Union Cause in St. Louis*, 301.

460. Chernow, *Grant*, 147.

461. Schofield, *Forty-Six Years in the Army*, 101.

462. Rombauer, *Union Cause in St. Louis*, 307; Schofield, *Forty-Six Years in the Army*, 85.

463. McFeely, *Grant*, 89.

464. Gerteis, *Civil War St. Louis*, 149.

465. Goodwin, *Team of Rivals*, 390.

466. Foner, *Fiery Trial*, 177, 179; Goodwin, *Team of Rivals*, 390–91.

467. Foner, *Fiery Trial*, 177; Chernow, *Grant*, 146.

468. Foner, *Fiery Trial*, 177; Goodwin, *Team of Rivals*, 392.

469. Goodwin, *Team of Rivals*, 392–93.

470. Parrish, *Frank Blair*, 119–20.

471. Goodwin, *Team of Rivals*, 393.

472. Parrish, *Frank Blair*, 119.

473. Goodwin, *Team of Rivals*, 393; Parrish, *Frank Blair*, 126. The second time he had Frank Blair arrested, Frémont imprisoned him at Jefferson Barracks.

474. Parrish, *Frank Blair*, 125.

475. Gerteis, *Civil War St. Louis*, 147; Parrish, *Frank Blair*, 125.

476. Goodwin, *Team of Rivals*, 395.

477. Ibid., 396.

478. Engle, *Yankee Dutchman*, 88–89; Parrish, *Frank Blair*, 130.

479. Winter, *Civil War in St. Louis*, 73.

480. Gerteis, *Civil War St. Louis*, 148.

481. Goodwin, *Team of Rivals*, 659–60.

Chapter 33

482. Engle, *Yankee Dutchman*, 26.

483. Ibid., 25–33.

484. Engle, *Yankee Dutchman*, 42; Winter, *Civil War in St. Louis*, 103.

485. Engle, *Yankee Dutchman*, 43.

486. Rombauer, *Union Cause in St. Louis*, 128.

487. Engle, *Yankee Dutchman*, 43.

488. Winter, *Civil War in St. Louis*, 103.

489. Engle, *Yankee Dutchman*, 44.

490. Gerteis, *Civil War St. Louis*, 85.

491. Ibid., 89.

492. Rombauer, *Union Cause in St. Louis*, 307.

493. Ibid., 311.

494. Rombauer, *Union Cause in St. Louis*, 313, 317; Schofield, *Forty-Six Years in the Army*, 89.

495. Rombauer, *Union Cause in St. Louis*, 326.
496. Ibid., 323.
497. Parrish, *Frank Blair*, 117.
498. Rombauer, *Union Cause in St. Louis*, 330; Parrish, *Frank Blair*, 111.
499. Parrish, *Frank Blair*, 112–13.
500. Rombauer, *Union Cause in St. Louis*, 333.
501. Engle, *Yankee Dutchman*, 78–82.
502. Rombauer, *Union Cause in St. Louis*, 334–35.
503. Engle, *Yankee Dutchman*, 101–2.
504. Ibid., 93–95.
505. Ibid., 148.
506. Ibid., 55.

Chapter 34

507. Schofield, *Forty-Six Years in the Army*, 69; *Kennedy's St. Louis Directory*, 1860.
508. Cain, *Lincoln's Attorney General Edward Bates*, 67.
509. Sinisi, *Sacred Debts*, 42.
510. Schofield, *Forty-Six Years in the Army*, 66.
511. Ibid., 70–1.
512. Ibid., 72.
513. Parrish, *Frank Blair*, 96.
514. Ibid.
515. Schofield, *Forty-Six Years in the Army*, 74.
516. Ibid., 76.
517. Ibid., 78.
518. Ibid., 99–100.
519. Ibid., 102.
520. Ibid., 112–13.
521. Ibid., 116.
522. Ibid., 117.
523. Ibid., 173–74.
524. Ibid., 117–19.
525. Ibid., 115, 123.
526. Ibid., 123, 132.
527. Ibid., 135–36.
528. Ibid., 140.
529. Ibid., 144–46.

530. Ibid., 184.
531. Ibid., 201.
532. Ibid., 473.

BIBLIOGRAPHY

Anderson, Galusha. *The Story of a Border City during the Civil War*. Boston: Little, Brown, 1908.

Arenson, Adam. "Building Union from Neutrality. St. Louis and the Cultural Civil War." *Gateway* 31 (2011): 23–30.

———. *The Great Heart of the Republic: St. Louis and the Cultural Civil War*. Columbia: University of Missouri Press, 2015.

Bartey, Mary. *St. Louis Lost*. St. Louis, MO: Virginia Publishing, 1994.

Basler, Roy B., ed. *The Collected Works of Abraham Lincoln*. New Brunswick, NJ: Rutgers University Press, 1953–55.

Bellamy, Donnie D. "Free Blacks in Antebellum Missouri, 1820–1860." *Missouri Historical Review* 67 (January 1973): 198–226.

———. "The Persistency of Colonization in Missouri." *Missouri Historical Review* 72, no. 1 (October 1977): 1–24.

Blackett, R.J.M. *The Captive's Quest for Freedom: Fugitive Slaves, the 1850 Fugitive Slave Law, and the Politics of Slavery*. Cambridge, UK: Cambridge University Press, 2018.

Bloomberg, Kathryn Elizabeth. "Charitable Women: Volunteerism in the St. Louis Ladies Union Aid Society." University of Missouri St. Louis Thesis 167, 2009. http://irl.umsl.edu/thesis/167.

Boernstein, Henry. *Memoirs of a Nobody: The Missouri Years of an Austrian Radical, 1849–1866*. St. Louis: Missouri Historical Society Press, 1997.

Brown, William Wells. *Narrative of William W. Brown, a Fugitive Slave*. Boston: Anti-Slavery Office, 1847.

Cain, Marvin R. *Lincoln's Attorney General Edward Bates of Missouri*. Columbia: University of Missouri Press, 1965.

"The Camp Jackson Incident." *Museum Gazette*. Jefferson National Expansion Memorial, May 1999.

Chernow, Ron. *Grant*. New York: Penguin Books, 2017.

"The City Class Ironclads." Vicksburg National Military Park. National Park Service. nps.gov.

Civil War Centennial Commission. *The Civil War in Missouri, 1861–1865* Jefferson City: Missouri State Parks, 1961.

Compton, Richard J., and Camille N. Dry. *Pictorial St. Louis: The Great Metropolis of the Mississippi Valley. A topographical survey drawn in perspective A.D. 1875*. Reprinted: St. Louis, McGraw-Young Publishing, 1997.

Cosner, Victoria, and Lorelei Shannon. *Missouri's Mad Doctor McDowell*. Charleston, SC: The History Press, 2015.

Davis, Jane. "Contraband Camps in St. Louis: A Contested Path to Freedom," *Confluence* (Fall/Winter 2011): 18–29.

Delaney, Lucy. *From the Darkness Cometh the Light, or Struggles for Freedom* (St. Louis, MO: J.T. Smith Publishing, 1891). Documenting the American South. https://docsouth.unc.edu.

Denver Post. "An Underground Railway Story." Reprinted in the *Minneapolis Journal*, July 4, 1901. https://www.newspapers.com.

Dickson, Moses. *Manual of the International Order of the Twelve of Knights and Daughters of Tabor, Containing General Laws, Regulations, Ceremonies, Drill and a Taborian Lexicon*. 1891. Northern Illinois University Digital Library. digital. lib.niu.edu.

Duke, Basil W. *Reminiscences*. Garden City, NY: Doubleday, Page & Company, 1911.

Dunson, A.A. "Notes on the Missouri Germans on Slavery," *Missouri Historical Review* 59, no. 3 (April 1965): 355–66.

Durst, Dennis L. "The Reverend John Berry Meachum (1789–1854) of St. Louis: Prophet and Entrepreneurial Black Educator." *The North Star: A Journal of African American Religious History* 7, no. 2 (Spring 2004), https://www.princeton.edu.

Edward's Annual Directory. St. Louis: Richard Edwards, 1864. http://digital.wustl.edu.

———. St. Louis: Richard Edwards, 1865. http://digital.wustl.edu.

———. St. Louis: Richard Edwards, 1866. http://digital.wustl.edu.

———. St. Louis: Richard Edwards, 1867. http://digital.wustl.edu.

Eiland, Sarah. "The Unspoken Demand of Slavery: The Exploitation of Female Slaves in the Memphis Slave Trade." *Rhodes Historical Review* 20 (Spring 2018): 43–62.

Engle, Stephen D. *Yankee Dutchman: The Life of Franz Sigel.* Fayetteville: University of Arkansas Press, 1993.

Faherty, William Barnaby, SJ. *Exile in Erin.* St. Louis: Missouri Historical Society Press, 2002.

Fardell, Joseph A. "Letter to Father and Mother, February 6, 1864." Missouri Historical Society. St. Louis, Missouri. http://collections.mohistory.org.

Flood, Charles Bracelen. *Grant and Sherman, the Friendship That Won the Civil War.* New York: Farrar, Straus and Giroux, 2005.

Floyd, John B. "Dispatch to Major Bell, US Arsenal. St. Louis, Missouri. November 25, 1860." Item number 170162. Missouri Historical Society. St. Louis, Missouri.

Foner, Eric. *The Fiery Trial: Abraham Lincoln and American Slavery.* New York: W.W. Norton, 2010.

Forest Park Statues and Monuments. http://www.forestparkstatues.org.

Frazier, Harriet C. *Slavery and Crime in Missouri, 1773–1865.* Jefferson, NC: McFarland, 2001.

"Freedom Suits." Gateway Arch National Park. National Park Service. https://www.nps.gov.

Gerteis, Louis S. *Civil War St. Louis.* Lawrence: University Press of Kansas, 2001

Goodwin, Doris Kearns. *Team of Rivals: The Political Genius of Abraham Lincoln.* New York: Simon & Schuster, 2005.

Green's St. Louis Business Directory 1845. St. Louis: J. Green and Cathcart & Prescott, 1845. Washington University Libraries. Digital Gateway. http//digital.wustl.edu.

———. St. Louis: J. Green and Cathcart & Prescott, 1847. http//digital.wustl.edu.

———. St. Louis: J. Green and Cathcart & Prescott, 1850. University of Missouri at St. Louis. Mercantile Library. https://dl.mospace.umsystem.edu.

Green's St. Louis Business Directory 1851. St. Louis: J. Green and Cathcart & Prescott, 1851. http//digital.wustl.edu.

Grissom, Daniel. "Personal Recollections of Distinguished Missourians." *Missouri Historical Review* 19, no.1 (October 1924): 94–98.

Hall, J.P. *The Early Developmental History of Concrete Block in America.* Muncie, IN: Ball State University, 2009. https://cardinalscholar.bsu.edu.

Hamilton, Esley. "Edward Bates and Grape Hill." *Society of Architectural Historians Missouri Valley Chapter Newsletter* 15, no. 3 (Fall 2009): 5–7.

———. "A New Picture on Glass of the Brant Mansion," *Society of Architectural Historians Missouri Valley Chapter Newsletter* 15, no. 3 (Fall 2009): 2–4.

Hamm, Thomas D. "A Quaker View of Black St. Louis in 1841." *Missouri Historical Review* 98, no. 2 (January 2004): 115–20.

Harding, Samuel B. *Life of George R. Smith, Founder of Sedalia, Mo.* Indianapolis, IN: Hollenback Press, 1904.

Hart, Jim A. "The *Missouri Democrat, 1852–1860.*" *Missouri Historical Review* 55, no. 2 (January 1961): 127–41.

Hartley, Edward. "Letter to Miss Em, September 8, 1862." Missouri Historical Society. St. Louis, Missouri. http://collections.mohistory.org.

Herman, Janet S. "The McIntosh Affair," *Missouri Historical Society Bulletin* 26 (January 1970): 123–43.

"Historic Jefferson Barracks." Missouri Civil War Museum. mcwm.org.

Hoffman, Judy. "If I Fall, My Grave Shall Be in Alton." *Gateway Heritage* 25, no. 4 (Spring 2005): 10–19.

Huling, Polly. "Missourians at Vicksburg," *Missouri Historical Review* 50, no. 1 (October 1955): 1–15.

An Illustrated History of the Missouri Botanical Garden. St. Louis: Missouri Botanical Garden. http://www.mobot.org/mobot/archives.

Johnson, Patty. "Founder's Day 2011 in St. Louis." *US Federation of the Sisters of St. Joseph* (blog), October 15, 2011. http://sistersofstjosephfederation. blogspot.com.

Joiner, Gary. *Mr. Lincoln's Brown Water Navy: The Mississippi Squadron.* Lanham, MD: Rowman & Littlefield, 2007.

Journal and Proceedings of the Missouri State Convention Held at Jefferson City and St. Louis. St. Louis, MO: George Knapp & Company, 1861.

Journal of the Missouri State Convention. St. Louis, MO: I.N. Henry and Company, 1820.

Keemle's St. Louis Directory for the Years 1836–37. St. Louis, MO: C. Keemle, 1836. University of Missouri Digital Library. St. Louis Mercantile Library. https://dl.mospace.umsystem.edu.

Keemle's St. Louis Directory for the Years 1838–39. St. Louis, MO: C. Keemle, 1838. http://digital.wustl.edu/cty1838.0001.005.

Keemle's St. Louis Directory for the Years 1840–41. St. Louis, MO: C. Keemle, 1840. http://digital.wustl.edu/cty1840.0001.006.

Kelly, Kevin. "MCC Assembly: Priest Lauds Civil War Bishops." *Catholic Key*, October 6, 2011. https://catholickey.org.

Kennedy's St. Louis Directory. St. Louis: R.V. Kennedy & Co., 1857. http:// digital.wustl.edu.

———. St. Louis, MO: R.V. Kennedy & Co., 1859. http://digital.wustl.edu.

———. St. Louis, MO: R.V. Kennedy & Co., 1860. http://digital.wustl.edu.

Kiner, F.F. *One Year's Soldiering: Embracing the Battles of Fort Donelson and Shiloh.* Lancaster, PA: E.H. Thomas, 1863.

Laughlin, Bonnie E. "Endangering the Peace of Society: Abolitionist Agitation and Mob Reaction in St. Louis and Alton, 1836–1838." *Missouri Historical Review* 95, no. 1 (October 2000): 1–22.

Livingston, Samuel. "An African Life of Resistance: Moses Dickson, the Knights of Liberty and Militant Abolitionism, 1824–1857." 2008. www.academia. edu/1600054/_Moses_Dickson_Militant_Abolitionist_1824-1865.

Lovejoy, Elijah. "Awful Murder and Savage Barbarity." *St. Louis Observer* May 5, 1835.

"Lucas Place in a Nutshell." Campbell House Museum. http://www. campbellhousemuseum.org.

Mason, David C. "Famous for Freedom Suits." Twenty-Second Circuit Court of Missouri, https://mohistory.org/blog/famous-for-freedom-suits.

McDowell, Joseph N. "Letter to Henry Ward Beecher." *Morning Herald*, December 18, 1859. Reprinted in Cosner and Shannon, *Missouri's Mad Doctor McDowell.*

McElroy, John. *The Struggle for Missouri.* Washington, DC: The National Tribune Company, 1909. Project Gutenberg eBook.

McFeely, William. *Grant.* New York: W.W. Norton, 1982.

Milligan, John. *Gunboats Down the Mississippi.* Annapolis, MD: United States Naval Institute, 1965.

Missouri Democrat, 1855, 1863. Microfilm at St. Louis Public Library Central Library.

Missouri Republican, 1855, 1863. Microfilm at St. Louis Public Library Central Library.

Missouri State Archives. "Before Dred Scott: Freedom Suits in Antebellum Missouri." Missouri Digital Heritage. Missouri Secretary of State. https://www.sos.mo.gov.

———. "Dred Scott Case, 1846–1857." Missouri Digital Heritage. Missouri Secretary of State. https://www.sos.mo.gov.

———. "Laws of Missouri, 1843." Missouri Digital Heritage. Missouri Secretary of State. Missouri Digital Heritage. https://www.sos.mo.gov.

———. "Laws of Missouri, 1847." Missouri Digital Heritage. Missouri Secretary of State. Missouri Digital Heritage. https://www.sos.mo.gov.

———. "Missouri's Early Slave Laws: A History in Documents." Missouri Secretary of State. Missouri Digital Heritage. https://www.sos.mo.gov.

Moore, Robert, Jr. "A Ray of Hope, Extinguished." *Gateway Heritage* 14, no. 3 (Winter 1993–94): 4–11.

Morrison's St. Louis Directory 1852. *Missouri Republican* (St. Louis, MO), 1852. http://digital.wustl.edu/cty/1852.0001.012.

New York Times. "The Proceedings of the First Day. Detailed Report from the Charleston Papers." April 27, 1860.

"Original plattings of forts at St. Louis, Mo. 186-." Corps of Engineers. United States Army. Library of Congress. https://www.loc.gov.

Parrish, William E. *Frank Blair, Lincoln's Conservative.* Columbia: University of Missouri Press, 1998.

Paxton, William. *Annals of Platte County, Missouri.* Kansas City, MO: Hudson-Kimberly Publishing, 1897.

Peterson, Norma. "The Political Fluctuations of B. Gratz Brown: Politics in a Border State, 1850–1870." *Missouri Historical Review* 60, no. 1 (October 1956): 22–30.

"Petitions to Leave to Sue for Freedom." Revised Dred Scott Case Collection. Washington University Libraries. Digital Gateway. http://digital.wustl.edu.

Phillips, Christopher. "The Radical Crusade: Blair, Lyon, and the Advent of Civil War in Missouri." *Gateway Heritage* 10, no. 4 (Spring 1990): 22–38.

Poole-Jones, Katherine. "Historical Memory, Reconciliation, and the Shaping of the Post-bellum Landscape: The Civil War Monuments of Forest Park, St. Louis." *Panorama* (Spring 2020). editions.lib.umn.edu/panorama.

Reavis, L.U., and Cassius Marcellus Clay. *The Life and Military Services of Gen. William Selby Harney.* St. Louis, MO: Bryan, Brand & Co, 1878.

Ritter, Luke. "The St. Louis Know-Nothing Riots of 1854." *Gateway* 32 (2012): 27–31.

Roberts, Anna K. "Crossing Jordan: The Mississippi River in the Black Experience in Greater St. Louis, 1815–1860." *Missouri Historical Review* 113, no. 1 (October 2018): 22–40.

Roe, Jason. "Missouri Rejects Secession." Civil War on the Western Border. Kansas City Public Library, https://civilwaronthewesternborder.org.

Rombauer, Robert Julius. *The Union Cause in St. Louis in 1861: An Historical Sketch.* St. Louis, MO: Nixon-Jones Printing Company, 1909.

Romeo, Sharon Elizabeth. "Freedwomen in Pursuit of Liberty: St. Louis and Missouri in the Age of Emancipation." PhD thesis, University of Iowa, 2009. https://doi.org/10.17077/etd.d22c9xt4.

Rosecrans, William. "General Order No. 65." *War of the Rebellion: A Compilation of the Official Records of the Union and Confederate Armies* (Washington, D.C., 1880–1901), series 1, vol. 34, part 3: 345–46.

Saint Louis Directory for the Year 1842. St. Louis, MO: Chambers & Knapp, 1842. http://digital.wustl.edu/cty1842.0001.007.

Saint Louis Directory for the Years 1854–5. St. Louis, MO: Chambers & Knapp, 1854. http://digital.wustl.edu/cty1854.0001.014.

Schofield, John. *Forty-Six Years in the Army*. New York: Century Co., 1897. Project Gutenberg eBook.

———. "Response to Letter from Pierre Berthold to Col. William Wood, Missouri State Militia, April 1, 1862." Berthold Family Papers. Missouri Historical Society. St. Louis, Missouri.

Schwarzbach, F.S. "The Burning of Francis L. McIntosh: A Note to a Dickens Letter from American." *Dickens Studies Newsletter* 11, no. 2 (1980): 38–41. http://www.jstor.org/stable/45290703.

Seematter, Mary E. "Trials and Confessions: Race and Justice in Antebellum St. Louis." *Gateway Heritage* 12, no. 2 (Fall 1991): 36–46.

Shipley, Alberta D. *History of Black Baptists in Missouri*. Kansas City: Missionary Baptists State Convention of Missouri, 1976.

Sinisi, Kyle S. *Sacred Debts, State Civil War Claims and American Federalism, 1861–1880*. New York: Fordham University Press, 2003.

Sneddeker, Duane, et al. National Register of Historic Places Nomination Form. Carondelet East of Broadway, St. Louis, Multiple Resource Area. 1979. https://mostateparks.com.

Stevens, George. *History of Central Baptist Church*. St. Louis, MO: King Publishing, 1927.

Stillwell, Leander. *The Story of a Common Soldier of Army Life in the Civil War 1861–1865*. Kansas City, MO: Franklin Hudson Publishing, 1920.

St. Louis American. "Central Baptist Church Celebrates 170th Anniversary." April 7, 2016.

St. Louis Circuit Court. "Historical Records Project." Washington University Libraries. Digital Gateway. digital.wustl.edu.

———. "St. Louis Mechanics Liens." Office of the Circuit Clerk. mdh.contentdm.oclc.org/digital/collection/stlmeclien.

St. Louis Daily Evening News, 1863.

St. Louis: Our Civil War Heritage. St. Louis, MO: Daughters of Union Veterans of the Civil War, 1861–1865. Julia Dent Grant Tent, #16, July 1992.

St. Louis Post-Dispatch. "Grant in St. Louis," March 14, 1885.

———. "Homes of Heroes Falling in St. Louis beneath Irreverent Hands." November 9, 1902.

———. "Life's Fitful Fever O'er: The Death of Gen. George P. Dorriss Last Night." November 30, 1882.

———. "One of Grant's Lounging Places." September 16, 1894.

———. "Russell Brown: The Youthful Slayer of His Grandmother Pleads Guilty to Manslaughter." March 26, 1883.

———. "Tom Dorris Dead." March 15, 1895. https://www.newspapers.com.

St. Louis Star and Times. "This Was St. Louis Slave Market Before Civil War." January 30, 1922. https://www.newspapers.com.

Straight, David L. "The Iowa Boys Winter in St. Louis, 1861–1862." *Confluence* (Spring/Summer 2011): 52–59.

"Suits for Freedom, St. Louis, 1804–1865." National Park Service. https://home.nps.gov.

Thompson, L.S. *The Story of Mattie J. Jackson: Her Parentage—Experience of Eighteen Years in Slavery—Incidents During the War—Her Escape from Slavery. A True Story. As Given by Mattie.* Lawrence, MA: Sentinel Office, 1866. https://docsouth.unc.edu.

VanderVelde, Lea. *Mrs. Dred Scott: A Life on Slavery's Frontier.* New York: Oxford University Press, 2009.

Wayne, Allen. "Establishing a Metropolitan Police Force, The Civil War and the First St. Louis Board of Police Commissioners." *Gateway Heritage* 19, no. 4 (Spring 1999): 30–36.

Westerman, Kim. "The Congregation Confronts Racism." *Carondelet Magazine* (May 1, 2020). https://csjcarondelet.org.

"W.G. Letter to Dear Brother, Camp Jackson, St. Louis, May 9, 1861." Missouri Historical Society. St. Louis, Missouri. Identifier: A0286-00055.

Williams, Scott. "U.S. Colored Troops and the Plight of the Refugee Slave." USGenNet. usgennet.org/usa/mo/county/stlouis/ct.htm.

Winter, William. *The Civil War in St. Louis.* St. Louis: Missouri Historical Society Press, 1995.

Wright, John. *Discovering African American St. Louis.* St. Louis: Missouri Historical Society Press, 2002.

Wright, John, and Sylvia Wright. *Extraordinary Black Missourians, Pioneers, Leaders, Performers, Athletes, & Other Notables Who've Made History.* St. Louis, MO: Reedy Press, 2013.

INDEX

ABOUT THE AUTHOR

Peter Downs is a writer in St. Louis, Missouri. He lives with his wife in a 150-plus-year-old house in the historic Soulard neighborhood, Ulysses S Grant's former neighborhood and the heart of the Unionist Home Guard movement in the Civil War.